HOW TO JUDGE
TRACK EVENTS

by David Littlewood

First published	W. C. Jewell	1950
Second edition	W. C. Jewell	1954
Third edition	W. C. Jewell	1958
Reprinted	W. C. Jewell	1962
Reprinted	W. C. Jewell	1964
Fourth edition	V. C. Sealy	1967
Fifth edition	D. C. Davies	1976
This edition	D. R. Littlewood	1995

ISBN 0 85134 129 2   2K/26K/06.95

© British Athletic Federation
225A Bristol Road, Birmingham B5 7UB

Designed and printed in England on 100gsm Huntsman Blade Cartridge by BPC Whitefriars Ltd., Tunbridge Wells, Kent TN2 3EN.

Contents

Photographs

Photofinish by courtesy of Seiko. All other photographs by David Littlewood.

About the Author

David Littlewood recently retired as Deputy Headmaster of Isleworth and Syon School in Hounslow in order to take up the duties of Honorary Secretary of the English Schools' Athletic Association. He has been Honorary Treasurer of Hercules Wimbledon Athletic Club for over 30 years and was elected President of the South of England Athletic Association in 1994.

He first qualified as both a Track and Field official in 1957 whilst at University, but has concentrated on Track Judging since those early days. Since 1981 he has been Honorary Secretary of the AAA/BAF Rules Revision Committee, and Chairman of the AAA/BAF Officials' Committee. He is also a member of the BAF Drugs Advisory Committee.

As an official, David Littlewood was appointed Track Referee in 1975 and has gained a wide experience at all levels of competition. He was Referee for the European Junior Championships in 1987, the European Cup Finals of both 1989 and 1994 and the World Student Games in 1991. He also had the privilege of refereeing the English Schools' Championships for 17 years.

On a broader front he has officiated at eight World Championships, three Commonwealth Games and the Barcelona Olympics, primarily in the area of photo finish. He was also appointed as International Technical Official at both the European Junior Championships in 1993 and the European Championships in 1994 and has successfully organised officials' courses for the IAAF abroad. He was one of the two British members of the new panel of International Technical Officials approved by the IAAF Council in November 1994.

INTRODUCTION

It may seem strange that such an apparently simple task as track judging should necessitate a booklet of this length! To many the job merely consists of writing down the finishing order at the end of a race, but there is far more to it than just placing up to eight competitors approaching you at speeds in excess of 20 mph in their correct finishing order, although this can be at times a daunting task. As a track official you must also be aware of the numerous rules which need to be obeyed by the athletes in their progress from the start to the finishing line, and how you can best position yourself to confirm whether these rules have been observed.

What are the requirements needed to become a successful Track Official? Above all else, you must possess the ability to divorce yourself from any considerations other than your particular duty. A high degree of concentration therefore is essential, as is the ability to work quickly and accurately under pressure. You are also a member of a team of officials and such a team can only work efficiently if well-led and if all members play their part. As with all officiating, a sense of humour is an essential requirement on those bitterly cold "summer" days, or as the rain slowly runs down your neck as you struggle with multiple lapping in a long distance race. Yet there is great satisfaction to be had from feeling that you have contributed to the smooth running of a meeting at whatever level. Certainly do not consider track officiating if you are expecting to receive the plaudits of the athletes for a job well done. Unlike our counterparts in the field events, there is usually very little contact between the track officials and the individual athletes. You will merely be one of the faceless group of officials located at the finish — until you have to deal with a protest or disqualify one of the competitors.

The main duties of a track official can be divided into two distinct activities, which may be generally described as Judging and Umpiring. When the official is acting as a Judge he or she is concerned with the finishing order of the race, the particular activity differing somewhat depending on the length of the race concerned. When acting as an Umpire the official is not concerned in any way with the result, but solely on whether the athletes are running the race in accordance with the Rules. These two functions require different techniques and will be dealt with separately here. Increasingly at major meetings the task of operating the wind gauge falls to one of the members of the track team, so this activity is also outlined within these pages. Similarly, photofinish is being used more frequently at meetings below international level and the opportunity has been taken to give a brief introduction to this whole area of activity.

Within this booklet the main emphasis will be on the interpretation of the Rules for Competition of the British Athletic Federation (BAF), but reference will also be made to the Rules of the International Amateur Athletic Federation (I.A.A.F.) which govern meetings at which foreign athletes compete and which differ in some important respects from the domestic rules. The BAF Rules for Competition are always being reviewed and revised, and you are strongly urged to obtain a copy of the current Rulebook of the BAF which should be read in conjunction with the information contained here.

CHAPTER 1

JUDGING

What is required

Under normal circumstances a judge operating on the stand at the finish of a race will be expected to place all of the competitors in order. To undertake this accurately in a sprint race requires practice and a high level of concentration. Strangely enough, in some middle distance races the finishes may be even more demanding of the judges if athletes slow down, anticipating that they are in a qualifying position for the final, only to be caught, often "on the line", by the chasing group.

To achieve an accurate result the judge must be able to absorb a great deal of information without becoming flustered. The judge needs to be able to take a mental picture of the finish and then translate this into competition numbers. This means that the judge must be able to ignore any distractions which may occur. If an athlete crashes to the ground at the final flight of hurdles it is all too easy to become concerned with his or her welfare rather than the result of the race. Above all, the judge must be completely divorced from any emotional involvement in the result of the race. Most leading judges would be unable to tell you the result of a race without reference to the competitors' numbers on their board. As a school-teacher I have often surprised my own athletes by asking them where they finished in a race I had just judged!

If there are sufficient judges available the Referee may designate one judge, or more, to be concerned only with the last three or four competitors in a sprint race. This is a useful safety measure. If there is a very close finish between the leading athletes, the judges' attention may be focussed on sorting out this result and the latter part of the field will only

be viewed scantily. Although this may seem a simpler option than placing all of the competitors in the race, it is usually the most demanding task you can be asked to cover as it involves allowing perhaps half of the field to pass before you spring into action. It only requires a close finish between athletes in the middle of the field to make the task of deciding when you should start judging your places a very difficult one indeed.

It is critical at this stage to underline what the judge is concerned with at the finish of the race. The distance of the race is measured from the edge of the start line furthest from the finish to the edge of the finish line nearest to the start. So, although the finish line is 5 cm wide, the athlete has completed the race when any part of the torso (i.e. as distinguished from the head, neck, arms, legs, hands or feet) *reaches* the vertical plane of the leading edge of the finish line. (Rule 113.3) An athlete falling headlong on the ground before the line has finished if any part of the torso so much as touches the leading edge of the line. The athlete may not literally "cross the line" but will still be deemed to have completed the race.

How to achieve it

How do the judges set about placing the athletes in the correct order? Firstly, by ensuring that they have a clear view of the finish. Assuming that there is a tiered stand at the finish line, it is essential that this is carefully located. It must be in direct line with the finish and should be as far back from the inside edge of the track as is possible. The Rules of the IAAF (Rule 118.2) suggest that the stand should be at least 5 metres from the edge of the track and this is a useful guide. At many stadia the stand is placed virtually on the edge of the track and it is then all too easy to take up a position in which the judges end up missing the athlete in the inside lane who effectively runs below the line of vision.

Having placed the stand in a good position, it is essential to place yourself on the stand where you have a clear and uninterrupted view of the line. Too often one sees judges on the stand who are quite unable to see the finish line because of the height of the judge in front of them. The only way they can see the athletes is to move to one side from which viewpoint they will not be able to judge the positions as the athletes reach the line, which is critical to accuracy. Never be afraid to ask the judge in front of you to go further down the steps on the stand so that you can have that uninterrupted view, or offer to change places.

At some venues there may not be the luxury of a judges' stand available, and a measure of improvisation is called for, still with the intention of creating several levels of viewing which give all of the judges a clear sight of the finish line. Two chairs can provide three judges with a moderate vantage point provided that one is prepared to stand on the chair to judge. With a second judge standing between the chairs and the third sitting on the front one all should have an uninterrupted view of the finish, although obviously the low angle of all three will make accurate judging of a very close finish almost impossible.

It is important to remember to be fair to other judges by not always rushing up to the highest positions on the stand before each race. The higher your position the better view you have of the runners, and it is only fair that this advantageous position should be shared around in the course of the meeting. Several judges have obtained an unenviable reputation for selfishness in this particular respect and inexperienced judges should be aware of this potential fault. As a Referee I always insist that the judges taking the last three or four positions in a sprint race should take up a high position on the stand, bearing in mind the potential difficulty of the task involved, and I would certainly recommend this as good practice. It must also be recognised that the judges on the lower positions on the stand are at a distinct disadvantage, and anyone trying to judge at ground level will find the view of the runners in the outside lanes blocked by those in the nearest lanes in any close finish. It is one of the most important duties of the Referee to ensure that he or she does not allocate more officials to the task of judging than can be conveniently accommodated on the stand provided. I have seen even experienced International Referees allocate ten judges to record the finish order of a sprint race. Apart from complicating the task of compiling a result from such a diversity of boards, it is impossible for all of these judges to have a clear view of the finish line and their results cannot therefore be accurate. I would never allocate more than five judges, together with a Chief Judge, to record the result of a sprint race.

Having positioned yourself in line with the finish, how do you proceed? In sprint races which are run in lanes it is often a great help to write down the athletes' numbers in lane order before the race. This immediately familiarises you with the combination of numbers which you are going to have to record, and enables you to check the figures you have written down at the end with the original draw. In the case of a number which was obscured, it should be easy to identify which it is by reference to your draw.

You must decide your own strategy for preparing for the finish but many judges, myself included, adopt the habit of watching the athletes approaching the finish, identifying numbers, particularly of those who appear to be in the leading group, until the leaders are about 10 metres or so from the line. At that stage the attention should be directed to the finish line and a mental "photograph" taken of the finishing order. It is not advisable to follow the athletes right through to the line since this encourages a pre-judging of the finishing order. The angle you are viewing from often gives a misleading impression, suggesting that those athletes in the outer lanes are well ahead of the rest and this can cause panic when it becomes clear that this is not so. This is perhaps the most common fault exhibited by inexperienced judges and should be resisted at all costs.

With the head and eyes kept firmly on the finish line, you may then begin to write down the numbers of the athletes as they reach the leading edge of the line. Some judges write horizontally across the page when recording the order but this has certain disadvantages since it is often difficult to decide where one competitor's number ends and the next begins, and I would certainly recommend that numbers are written vertically down the page.

Where it is impossible to read an athlete's number card, write down anything which will enable you to identify the individual subsequently — an initial letter for the colour of the vest, or two lines to indicate a vest with hoops on it would normally be sufficient identification. (Do not attempt to identify the athlete by name). Avoid the common mistake of following that athlete through the finish line in an attempt to identify the number. You will then have diverted your eyes from the line and will not clearly see the remaining athletes reaching the line. It happens quite often that in a close finish the placing of the last few runners in the race is hopelessly inaccurate where the judges follow the runners past the finish. On returning their vision to the finish they are quite likely to accept that the order of the finish was the same as at a point a few metres past the line. Fast finishing athletes may therefore be given a higher placing than they deserve, whilst those who slow up dramatically as soon as the line is reached may find themselves penalised. It is in such circumstances that the judge recording only the last three or four athletes may be invaluable in averting such a mistake.

When you are certain that you have placed all of the competitors you are responsible for, carry out a quick check against the start numbers and ensure that all of your numbers are legible. It is essential at this stage that you do not discuss the result with any other judge nor look at any other boards for confirmation. If you are doubtful about a placing it is important to leave a clearly indicated gap in your result. The Referee will assume that you are confident about any result displayed and will have to operate on that information. Never be afraid to admit that you have not managed to place all of the competitors — this is much better than presenting an inaccurate or copied result. Having checked your result, this should be held up for inspection by the Referee who will normally be located on the top step of the judges' stand. (See page 23 for the role of the Referee in compiling a result from the judges' boards).

The ability to place up to eight athletes in a sprint race accurately is an acquired skill and an inexperienced judge should appreciate that this takes time to develop. Do not be discouraged if your early attempts at judging produce results which do not accord with other more experienced officials, even when the fields are small. After the result has been decided by the Referee, take the opportunity to discuss the finish with the other judges. Most will be quite happy to offer advice and encouragement.

What equipment do you need?

In order to judge efficiently you need relatively little equipment. A clipboard is an essential requirement, as is a supply of paper, preferably unlined. Some judges divide their page into clear columns in advance and this is useful if you are confident that you can write your numbers unseen within the confines of the lines provided. No matter what system you use, it is essential that you indicate what event the result relates to. If there is a query at a later stage you may need to refer back to your result for confirmation, and this becomes very difficult if you have sheets of paper with hastily written numbers but no way of identifying quickly to which race those numbers relate.

As far as writing equipment is concerned, avoid the temptation to use pens of any kind. Ball point or similar pens have an unfortunate habit of running out of ink at a critical moment, and if there is a sudden downpour of rain they may stop functioning completely, or the result may slowly be washed from your page as you watch! As your result will need to be read by the Referee from the top of the judges' stand it must be clearly legible from a distance. In order to achieve this a pencil with a fairly thick point should be used. These pencils tend to be fairly soft but give a clear impression and will write readily, even under quite adverse conditions. Avoid using a standard HB pencil since this will give only a fine line, not easily read from a distance, and will tend to cut into the paper should it become fairly wet. In very wet conditions you may find a 5B or 6B pencil preferable. I have used such pencils successfully even when rain water was running down the board, and they have continued to record without cutting the paper. It is a useful tip to sharpen your pencils at both ends since this will enable you to turn the pencil round if the point breaks during your recording of a result, although it is unusual for the pencils mentioned above to break during normal use.

Rain clearly is an unfortunate hazard which can rapidly affect the accuracy of a result. It is therefore essential to have a supply of large, stout, transparent plastic bags which will accommodate the clipboard and a hand clutching a pencil, without restricting the movement of that hand within the bag. There are on the market clipboards with transparent covers which provide some protection from the elements for the paper

and you may prefer to experiment with one of these rather than use plastic bags. Every effort should be made to present a result to the Referee which can still be read from a distance, even though shrouded in plastic!

It is important to protect your recording paper from the rain, but it is even more important to ensure that you are fully protected from the elements. No-one operates very efficiently when saturated, so it is essential to carry full protective clothing, preferably including boots or similar footwear, as well as additional warm clothing particularly for evening meetings. It is better to have carried these unnecessarily to twenty meetings rather than to regret their absence on the one occasion they are needed!

Specific judging duties

Lap scoring

Rule 112.4 requires the Referee to appoint at least one judge to record the laps covered by each competitor in events longer than 1500m. I normally designate one judge to undertake this task in Mile races, but for longer distances when the chance of athletes being lapped by the leaders increases a larger number will be needed to ensure accuracy. This duty requires both an element of preparation beforehand and intense concentration during the race. Most judges have a supply of already prepared sheets to suit their individual method and this is a useful addition to your pieces of equipment to carry to every meeting.

These sheets should be made out in columns, preferably arranged vertically with a heading above each column which indicates the number of laps remaining for the athlete at that point in the race. This should then correspond with the figure being displayed on the lap board. It is useful to have a space on the sheet to insert the numbers of the competitors who are on the start list and a careful count should be made of the total number of competitors who start. If the field is a large one, then it is advisable for the lap scorers to work in pairs with one calling out the numbers of the competitors whilst the other concentrates on writing these down in the appropriate column. It is essential that the judge writing concentrates solely on that task, rather than looking up from time to time to watch the progress of the race. It is likely that not all the competitors will be recorded over the first couple of laps or so if the field is very large or if there is a substantial leading group. Do not worry about this, but attempt certainly to identify as many of the leading athletes as possible, together with those who are towards the back of the field since these are the two groups of athletes you may well be particularly concerned with as the race progresses. Make a careful note of any athlete who drops out from the race. (An example of a lap scoring sheet is shown below).

If athletes are lapped by the leaders it is usual to mark this in a distinctive way on the recording sheet. There is no universal method for this, and you will be well advised to devise your own system which you maintain whenever you are lap scoring. Care must be taken when an athlete has been lapped more than once and appropriate symbols will need to be used to indicate this clearly on your sheet. It is advisable to label the penultimate column on your chart as "Bell" or "B" rather than "1" as a reminder to ensure that the judge in charge of the lap

board and bell is in position and ready to ring the bell to indicate the start of the last lap. The final result will obviously be recorded in the last column on the sheet. It is usual for the Referee to ask one of the lap scorers to call out the result recorded on that board whilst the others carefully check their result against this. It would obviously be a rather laborious task for the Referee to inspect each board in turn if there are a large number of finishers. If you disagree with any of the places called, wait until the judge has reached the end of the list before raising your objection.

In events held under IAAF Rules a different method of lap scoring should be used for events over 5000 metres and for all Walking events. (IAAF Rule 124). The Referee is required to appoint lap scorers who are responsible for no more than 4 athletes in the race (6 in Walking races) and these scorers record the times for each of their competitors at the end of every lap, these times being called out by an official timekeeper. Whilst this is a feasible proposition if dealing with fairly small numbers, it involves a very large number of officials if the field is sizeable, and for this reason this method is little used in this country. One obvious additional complication of this method is that no single judge has the complete result and this can only be obtained by a scrutiny of the final times recorded for each athlete. If two athletes cross the line with the same time there is no obvious way of identifying their final position relative to each other from these sheets.

MEETING:
EVENT :

DATE:
AGE GROUP:

	3000m		2000m					
STARTERS	7 to go	6 to go	5 to go	4 to go	3 to go	2 to go	BELL	RESULT

Fig. 1. Lap Scoring Sheet.

Lap board and bell

For all races in excess of one lap an official will be appointed to operate the lap scoring board and ring the bell to indicate the start of the last lap. This appears to be a simple task, but it is not without its potential pitfalls and requires the judge's undivided attention. The board should be placed 10 to 15 metres before the finish line. In races held over a number of laps it is usual for a lap scorer to be designated to assist the person operating the board, and to call or indicate to athletes who have been lapped how far they still have to go.

The lap board should always indicate the number of laps left for the leaders as they approach. The lap scorer should advise when the bell is to be rung for particular athletes, this constituting a service not only for the athlete, but also for the timekeepers who will be looking to time competitors in specific finishing positions. Where photofinish is in operation, a token ring of the bell for each competitor entering the final lap is also an invaluable aid.

It should be noted that the IAAF Rule 124.2 concerning the operation of the lap board was amended in 1994 and now instructs the official in charge to change the lap counter "when the leader enters the straight that ends at the finish line". Additionally, there is an instruction that "manual indication shall be given, when appropriate, to competitors who have been, or are about to be lapped." These changes are not thought appropriate to include in BAF Rules.

Care should always be taken when ringing the bell, especially for the leader(s), that the sound of the bell does not drown the intermediate times being called to the athletes by the appointed timekeeper. It is advisable, therefore, to ring the bell well before the athletes reach the finish line, stopping just as they pass the lap board, thereby leaving the timekeeper with undisturbed calling.

Team Scoring

Although team races are now held only infrequently on the track, the official must be aware of the method to be adopted to obtain a result. (Rules 8 & 100). There are two possible ways to produce a result and the method to be adopted has to be made clear to the athletes before the race starts. The result may be determined by adding together the times achieved in the race by each of the scoring members of the team, the team with the shortest overall time being declared the winner. More usually, though, the result is determined by the finishing positions of the athletes concerned, the team scoring the least number of points according to the positions in which the members of the team finish (whose positions are to count) being declared the winner. In compiling the result the positions of the non-scoring members of a team, whether it finishes all of its members or not, are used in computing the scores of the other teams.

In the case of a tie between two athletes in the race, the positions they would have occupied if they had finished in a file are added together and divided by two and each scores that total. (For example, if two athletes dead-heat for fourth place they each score 4.5 points for their team). If the teams are tied in total points the higher placing goes to the team whose last scoring member finishes nearest the first place.

An example of a team race result is given below:

5000 metres Team Race (Teams of 4 to run with 3 to score)

Competing teams: A B C D and E
Result

	Team			Team
1	B		11	A
2	A		12	B
3	C		13	C
4	D		14	D
5	C		15	C
6	D		16	D
7 =	E & B		17	E
9	A		18	B
10	A		19	E
			20	E

Team A scores: $2+9+10$	$=21$	points
Team B scores: $1+7.5+12$	$=20.5$	points
Team C scores: $3+5+13$	$=21$	points
Team D scores: $4+6+14$	$=24$	points
Team E scores: $7.5+17+19$	$=43.5$	points

Team Result

1. Team B   20.5 points
2. Team A   21   points   (Last scorer in 10th place)
3. Team C   21   points   (Last scorer in 13th place)
4. Team D   24   points
5. Team E   43.5 points

CHAPTER 2

UMPIRING

Very little knowledge of the Rules for Competition is needed if the official is acting as a Judge, but when that role changes to being an Umpire the situation is much different. To carry out duties as an Umpire effectively the official must be conversant with every Rule which relates to track running, and must be aware of the action which needs to be taken if it is observed that an athlete has infringed any of them.

It is perhaps important at the outset to note the IAAF Rule which declares Umpires to be "assistants to the Referee, without power to give decisions." (IAAF rule 119.1). The same is true for competitions held under BAF Rules. All the decisions taken as a result of the report of an Umpire are the direct responsibility of the Referee, so any information provided by the Umpire to the Referee must be both detailed and clear. Once again, this duty requires absolute concentration at all times since infringements can occur without warning and must be observed carefully and reported accurately.

Lane Umpiring

One of the most important duties of an Umpire is to check that athletes do not stray from their own lanes. This is true of events run wholly or partly in lanes. There is an important difference here between the Rules of the IAAF and those of the BAF, although this should not make any difference to the Umpire and what is reported. Under IAAF Rules (IAAF Rule 141.3) an athlete is automatically disqualified for running as little as one step on or over the inside line marking the boundary of the lane, when running round the bend, unless forced to do so by another competitor. An athlete will not be

disqualified for running out of lane in the straight as long as this does not impede the progress of another competitor since no advantage is gained, indeed the athlete is adding to the distance run. Nor will there be any penalty for running over the outside lane line around the bend unless, again, another athlete is impeded in the process.

Under domestic Rules (Rule 112.1) the onus lies with the Referee to decide whether an athlete has gained "a material advantage" by running out of lane around the bend. The current Rulebook contains a table which gives an indication of the advantage accruing to an athlete who runs out of lane, and this may well be useful in deciding whether the advantage gained by the athlete was "material". (See Table 1). This places on the Umpire the task of identifying how far out of the lane the athlete runs and for how many strides (which must be carefully recorded).

The Umpire will be allocated by the Referee a position on the track from which to view for infringements. These positions have been traditionally identified by the terms "Bend 1", "Bend 2", "Bend 3" and "Bend 4", Bends 1 and 2 being the two halves of the bend nearest to the finish, whilst Bends 3 and 4 are the two halves of the bend at the far end of the track. On occasions it may be necessary to ask an Umpire to cover the whole of a bend single-handed. In major meetings held under IAAF Rules the number of track officials appointed has been increased recently to take into account the mandatory disqualification for lane infringements around the bends. In order to facilitate accurate location of these Umpires most Referees now use a standard diagram which I produced following a National Officials' Conference some years ago (see Fig. 2 on page 9) and this may be useful no matter what the level of the competition. Although there are positions indicated both on the inside and the outside of the track, the best place to watch for lane

Table 1.

Track 400 metres Stride 2.30m Number of Strides	Advantage Gained by Encroaching *t* cm on Inside of Lane			
	t = 50 mm	*t* = 100 mm	*t* = 150 mm	*t* = 300 mm
	mm	mm	mm	mm
1	4	7	11	22
2	7	14	22	44
3	11	22	33	66
4	14	29	44	88
5	18	36	54	109
6	22	44	65	131
7	25	51	76	153
8	29	58	87	175
9	33	65	98	197
10	36	72	109	219

This table shows, mathematically, the theoretical advantage gained by taking from 1 to 10 strides inside the inner border of a lane. The distances are shown in millimetres, e.g. four strides 150 mm inside gives an advantage of 44 mm.

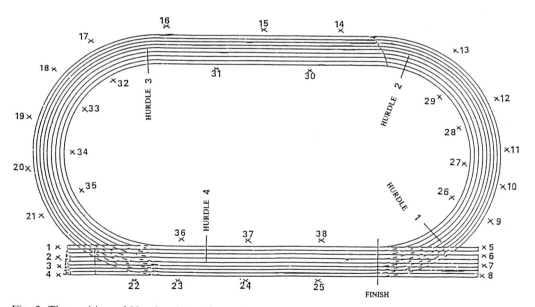

Fig. 2. The position of Umpires in track events.

infringements is on the outside where Umpires can look along the lane lines as they curve towards them. The photograph above shows the excellent view obtained from position 20.

One of the most important facts to bear in mind when umpiring on the bend is just what does constitute the athlete's lane. It is a common fallacy that the athlete is allowed to run on the line marking the inside of the lane, but not allowed to run on the one marking the outside, whereas the exact opposite is true. This is not as strange as it may appear at first sight, since the "line" marking the inside boundary of lane 1 is likely to be a concrete kerb approximately 5 cm high and does not allow the athlete

occupying that lane to run "on the line". The width of each lane is measured from the outside of the inner line to the outside of the outer line, so clearly the inner line is not part of the athlete's territory, whereas the outer line does fall within it.

It might be assumed that a clear understanding of the boundary of the lanes would be fundamental to all athletes and yet I well remember talking to one of the most famous and successful British athletes of recent years, a former European and Commonwealth champion, and in the course of conversation I bemoaned the introduction by the IAAF of the rule which provided for automatic disqualification if even one step was taken on the inside lane line. He expressed surprise and declared that he was glad that in his days of competing athletes were allowed to run on that line. His surprise was complete when I pointed out that it was only the punishment which had been altered; the restriction on the athlete had always been there! I, therefore, always instruct my Umpires to let athletes know that they have infringed an important rule, even when no action is to be taken as far as disqualification is concerned. Almost inevitably, the athletes concerned express surprise that such a rule exists as no-one had ever informed them of it!

As an Umpire you may also be asked to view lane running in the straight where you will be looking both for the position of the feet relative to the lane line and for the position of the body, especially the arms, relative to the runners in adjacent lanes. It is quite possible for an athlete to run within his or her lane but to fling arms sideways so that they impede or intimidate the athlete in an adjoining lane. As will be seen below, this is a particular problem in hurdle events, but it is not unknown in the closing stages of flat sprint races. As before, it is essential that the Umpire gives a clear account to the Referee as to what happened, even if the athletes themselves appear unconcerned.

In order to undertake this duty you may be asked to position yourself either behind the start line or beyond the finish line. If you are the only Umpire covering this duty you will need to take up a central position across the track so that you can see all of the lanes. More usually, though, this duty will be shared with other Umpires and you can quickly agree on an equitable distribution of the occupied lanes. If you are positioned behind the start you must ensure that you do not impede the vision of the Starter or Start Recaller, nor interfere with the work of the Marksmen. At the finish, you should be located well beyond the finish line so that you do not distract the attention of the approaching athletes.

Events run partly in lanes

On most tracks it is possible to hold 800 metre races with the first 130 metres or so run in lanes, as is also the case with the 4×400 metre relay. As an Umpire you may well be asked to oversee the Break Line to ensure that athletes do not leave their lanes before reaching the appropriate line. This is quite a difficult task especially if there are eight runners, but can be made even worse if you take up a poor viewing position. Too often I see even experienced international officials standing on the outer edge of the line itself to judge the "break". If you do take up such a position your view is likely to be obscured by runners in the outer lanes covering those in the inside, and you will be attempting to decide where the feet of up to eight athletes are relative to the lane lines which you are looking at sideways on. It is much better to take up a position on the outside of the track about 10 or so metres beyond the line, from where you will be able to observe the feet of the athletes as you look along the lane lines.

When carrying out this duty it is usual to have a pair of flags to indicate to the Referee whether the break has been successfully accomplished or not. Always ensure that you signal clearly and do not put the flag down until you have received an acknowledgement from the Referee or the Chief Judge that it has been seen. Where a break has been made prematurely you will need to note how far before the line the athlete left the lane, whether breaking early impeded any other athlete and whether the athlete made any attempt to regain the correct lane before reaching the line. All of this information will be needed by the Referee to decide whether a "material advantage" has been gained.

Obstruction

One of the most difficult infringements to identify and take action against is that of an athlete deliberately obstructing or pushing another in the course of a race. In any race in which the athletes are not running within the confines of their own lanes there is likely to be a certain amount of slight contact as athletes jockey for position, or close up together as the pace at the front slackens for any reason. Many athletes who fall to the track during a race are the victims of their own actions as they accidentally trip over the feet of those they are following too closely. In only a minority of cases is there likely to be a deliberate action which can be interpreted as an infringement of Rule 112.2 which states that "Any competitor jostling, running or walking across, or obstructing another competitor so as to impede his or her progress shall be liable to disqualification." It should be noted that disqualification is not mandatory even in those cases where an infringement is deemed to have occurred, and it is up to the Referee to decide whether the incident warrants disqualification or merely a warning.

In the distant past the domestic rule governing obstruction actually quoted two yards as the distance an athlete should be clear of another before moving to the inside. Although a figure is no longer given within the text of the rules, it is perhaps worth considering a metre or so as a reasonable guideline for the athlete to aim for, since this would enable the inside to be gained without any possibility of impedance. This is clearly another example of the need for very accurate reports from Umpires if the Referee is to make a fair decision, since it is likely that the officials at the finish will not have had a clear view of the incident.

In order to make a detailed report the Umpire must attempt to take up a position from which an infringement may be most readily observed. This is a difficult task since in a middle distance race with a large field it is often impossible to see all the athletes clearly, no matter where you stand. It is important to make yourself conspicuous to the athletes as this can often prove a useful deterrent. This is particularly true of the start of a race begun from a curved line. The presence of an official on the edge of the track some distance in front of the start line can have a positive effect on the field, and persuade the more vigorous to move with caution! On the whole, it is probably better to take up a position on the outside of the track, especially around bends, since this does provide a wider range of vision. The official should continue to follow the athletes around the track, even when they have moved away from the allocated umpiring position, since it is sometimes possible to see an infringement from behind which is hidden from other Umpires nearer to the incident.

Hurdles Events

Of all the possible umpiring duties perhaps those relating to hurdle events provide the most demanding challenge. There are so many different potential areas for infringements that the Umpire's concentration must be total and reports of incidents need to be clear and precise.

The Umpire does not only have to worry about infringements but must also be prepared and able to check that the hurdles have been placed in the right place, at the correct height and with an appropriate weighting. The official is not expected to carry details of the spacing between hurdles in the head, but many track judges carry the information on cards or in a small notebook. On tracks with a synthetic surface the hurdle positions are usually marked in a standard colour and groundsmen at cinder tracks are likely to follow the same sequence, details of which can be found in the table opposite. The Umpire is therefore likely to become familiar with most of the markings for standard hurdle events fairly quickly.

As with the track markings, the track official is likely to become familiar fairly quickly

Table 2. Specifications for Standard Hurdle Events under BAF Rules for Competition

Distance of race	Height of hurdle	Distance to 1st flight	Distance between flights	Distance to finish	Number of hurdles	Standard Track Marking Colour
MEN'S EVENTS						
Seniors (3.6 kg Toppling Weight)						
110 m	106.7 cm	13.72 m	9.14 m	14.02 m	10	Blue
400 m	91.4 cm	45 m	35 m	40 m	10	Green
Juniors (3.6 kg Toppling Weight)						
110 m	99.0 cm	13.72 m	9.14 m	14.02 m	10	Blue
200 m	76.2 cm	18.29 m	18.29 m	17.1 m	10	Purple
400 m	91.4 cm	45 m	35 m	40 m	10	Green
Under 17 (2.7 kg Toppling Weight)						
100 m	91.4 cm	13 m	8.5 m	10.5 m	10	Yellow
400 m	84.0 cm	45 m	35 m	40 m	10	Green
Under 15 (2.7 kg Toppling Weight)						
80 m	84.0 cm	12 m	8 m	12 m	8	Black
Under 13 (2.7 kg Toppling Weight)						
80 m	76.2 cm	12 m	8 m	12 m	8	Black
75 m	76.2 cm	11.5 m	7.5 m	11 m	8	Orange
WOMEN'S EVENTS						
Seniors and Juniors (3.6 kg Toppling Weight)						
100 m	84.0 cm	13 m	8.5 m	10.5 m	10	Yellow
400 m	76.2 cm	45 m	35 m	40 m	10	Green
Under 17 (2.7 kg Toppling Weight)						
80 m	76.2 cm	12 m	8 m	12 m	8	Black
100 m	76.2 cm	13 m	8.5 m	10.5 m	10	Yellow
200 m	76.2 cm	16 m	19 m	13 m	10	White
300 m	76.2 cm	50 m	35 m	40 m	7	Green
Under 15 (2.7 kg Toppling Weight)						
75 m	76.2 cm	11.5 m	7.5 m	11 m	8	Orange
Under 13 (2.7 kg Toppling Weight)						
70 m	68.5 cm	11 m	7 m	10 m	8	Pink

with the various hurdle heights for the standard events and these should be committed to memory. (See the table above). In order to be able to carry out such a check for height a small metal tape measure is a vital part of the equipment which should be carried at all times. (It should be remembered that there is a tolerance in manufacture allowed of 3 mm above and below the specified height so there will not always be a perfectly level top to a flight of hurdles).

Most hurdles sold today have built-in weights in the legs which enable the correct "toppling weight" for the height and age group to be set. The hurdle legs will probably initially have a label which will indicate the toppling weight and the height for each position, but if this has been removed the official can usually calculate the correct setting by working back from the position furthest from the hurdle bar which will represent a toppling weight of 3.6 kg and a hurdle height of 106.7 cms, i.e. the setting for the Senior Mens' 110 m Hurdles. One position forward from this will represent 3.6 kg at 99.0 cms, two forward 3.6 kg at 91.4 cms and so on.

In most cases the hurdles weights will also be calibrated to topple if a force of 2.7 kg is applied to the centre of the top of the cross-bar. This setting is the one to be used for competitions involving athletes in the Under 17 age group and below, and for some Veteran age groups. Again this information will normally be visible on the leg of the hurdle, but in its absence it should be assumed that the setting nearest the hurdle bar will represent a toppling weight of 2.7 kg and a hurdle height of 76.2 cms. From this it should again be possible to calculate the correct position for a given race and age group. (Unfortunately, there are some hurdles currently available from leading manufacturers which make no provision for a toppling weight of 2.7 kg and allow only five possible positions for the weights).

It is one of the duties of the Track Clerk of the Course to check the hurdles being used in a competition. The toppling weight can be checked most easily by fixing a simple spring balance to the centre of the hurdle bar and pulling until the hurdle legs leave the ground. This "toppling weight" can then be checked against a calibrated scale on the balance. The force exerted should fall between 3.6 and 4.0 kg (or 2.7 and 3.0 kg for younger age groups). The Table on page 13 gives the correct toppling weight for each of the hurdle events.

If the mechanics of setting up the hurdles appears to be complicated, this is but the prelude to the even more difficult task of umpiring the event! The Umpire has to be concerned with a number of basic rules which relate specifically to hurdling. Rule 116.12 summarises the main offences. "Competitors who trail a foot or leg below the plane of the top of the hurdle at the instant of clearance, or negotiate any hurdle not in their lane, or in the opinion of the Referee deliberately knock down any hurdle by hand or foot shall be disqualified." To these infringements should be added the question of possible obstruction (Rule 112.2) and running out of lane around a bend in the 200 m, 300 m and 400 m hurdle events (Rule 112.1).

I always find it rather disturbing at major championships abroad to see the umpires in 100 m and 110 m hurdle events placed alongside each flight of hurdles and usually seated throughout the event. Of the infringements noted above, only that relating to the deliberate taking down of a hurdle can be readily seen from such a position. For most of the other possible infringements a head-on position appears to me to be the best. If there are enough umpires available I would always place a number both behind the start and beyond the finish line. From this position hurdle clearances can easily be checked, as can most cases of obstruction. (See photograph on page opposite). Additional umpires placed alongside the track are valuable as a check on deliberate taking down of the hur-

dles, and they will also be able to add to the report on possible obstruction incidents as well.

With hurdle events run around the bend the exact positioning of the umpire should be left to the official's discretion. Again, if there are sufficient umpires available it is normal to allocate a flight of hurdles to each. In the early flights of these events the hurdles are spread over a considerable lateral distance and a position must be taken up which allows the umpire to have a clear sight of all eight hurdles. Although the umpire may have specific responsibility for a particular flight, it is good practice to follow the athletes over as many other flights as are clearly visible. The Referee will obviously welcome corroborating reports from a number of officials if a possible disqualification is involved.

Steeplechase Events (Rule 117)

Under domestic rules there are three standard steeplechase events which increase in distance as the age group advances:—

Under 17 Men compete over 1500 metres involving the clearance of 3 water jumps and 13 hurdles.

Junior Men (Under 20 Men) compete over 2000 metres, 5 water jumps and 18 hurdles.

The standard Senior event is run over 3000 metres, 7 water jumps and 28 hurdles.

At the time of writing, considerable discussion is taking place over the appropriate distances which women should run as their event begins to grow in popularity. Manufacturers are reviewing the design of steeplechase barriers in an attempt to produce a hurdle which is capable of being adjusted in height, since the standard height of 91.4 cm is considered too high both for women and, perhaps, the Under 17 Mens' age group.

It should be noted that the rules, at the time of writing, specifically bar athletes in the Under 15 and younger Boys' age groups from participating in ANY steeplechase event, as well as all women athletes below the Senior age group.

On the whole, the possible infringements in these events are similar to those which may occur in normal hurdle races and the regulations concerning the actual clearance of the barriers are identical. The major additional problem concerns the possibility of athletes impeding each other as they approach or actually clear the barriers, since obviously they are free to take up their own position on the track as they approach an obstacle. An official needs to bear this in mind when choosing a position from which to act as an umpire if given the responsibility for watching a barrier or the water jump. Whether the umpire chooses to locate inside or on the outside of the track, a position some distance down the track from the obstacle is essential so that the approach, the clearance and the movement away from the barrier can be clearly observed.

The water jump is a particularly hazardous barrier, for the athletes have to time their approach exactly to ensure that they can step onto the top of the hurdle cleanly before launching themselves across the 3.6 m of water. It is not permissible to place any kind of check mark alongside the approach to the water jump and the official(s) designated to watch the water jump should be aware of this restriction. The athletes do not have to clear the water and most will land with one foot in the shallow section near the end of the pool. It is an offence if an athlete leaps to one side or the other of the water but, as with all of the barriers in these events, it is quite permissible for the athletes to step on the top of the hurdle, or to use their hands to climb over them.

Care should always be taken to ensure that the hurdles and the water jump barrier are in good condition, being firmly placed on the track and without dangerous protrusions, and that the water jump is filled virtually to the top with water. Too often wooden hurdles are kept out in all weather conditions and will then rot, giving both a friable top and possibly uneven supports to the legs. Any such deficiencies should be reported immediately to the Referee who must then decide whether the event constitutes a danger to the competitors and should be cancelled.

Another point to bear in mind with

Table 3. Distances from start to first barrier to be cleared with an inside water jump.

	Age group	Number of hurdles	Number of water jumps	Distance from start to first hurdle
3000 m	Senior men	28	7	257.8 m
2000 m	Junior men	18	5	203.8 m
1500 m	Under 17 Men	13	3	255.8 m

steeplechase events is that not all of the barriers are placed on the track from the outset. In general, where the water jump is placed in its traditional position on the inside of the track, there is a run of at least 200 m before any barrier is cleared. The exact distances are given in Table 3. Where the water jump is placed on the outside of the standard track the distance between the start and the first barrier will be far less, the actual distances varying from track to track depending on the exact length of a lap including the water jump. It is important to bear this fact in mind when deciding what is an appropriate number of athletes to contest a steeplechase event. Where the distance to the first barrier to be cleared is particularly short it is desirable for that barrier to be of a greater width than standard and on many tracks, even where there is an "inside" water jump, this is becoming common practice.

Relay Races (Rule 118)

The traditional track programme ends with the relays and these provide another difficult task for the umpire. The basic rules are quite straightforward since the baton has to be passed from one athlete to another within a 20 metre take-over zone and this has to be achieved without impeding any other competitors. Different problems face the Umpire in dealing with the 4 × 100 m (which is always run in lanes) and longer events where only part of the race may be contested in lanes.

Whichever event is being run, the rules relating to the passing of the baton remain the same. It is vital that the Umpire appreciates that in deciding whether the passing of the baton has been effected within the 20 m take-over it is the position of the baton and not of the body of the athlete(s) which is of significance. It is quite possible for the outgoing athlete to have a foot well over the end of the take-over box but, with the arm and hand extended backwards, still receive the baton within the required zone. (To assist the hard-pressed official the rules recommend that batons are of distinctive colours which can make identifying the position of the baton a little easier). The passing of the baton is deemed to commence when it is first touched by the receiving runner and is completed the moment it is in the hand of the receiving runner only. Where the event is being run wholly or partly in lanes athletes may place a check mark on the track, but this may only be placed within the confines of their own lane. On synthetic surfaces athletes must be told to use adhesive tape rather than chalk or similar substances as their marker. Note also that an athlete is only allowed to place one check mark on the track.

Where the leg does not exceed 200 m the situation is further complicated by the option offered to the athletes to use an additional 10 m zone located before the actual take-over box. This is used by the athletes to gather speed so that they are travelling faster when the baton is passed. The passing of the baton within this "acceleration zone" is not allowed and brings automatic disqualification. The acceleration zone is always marked in a different colour to the actual take-over zone. I never point out this zone when dealing with very young athletes since few are aware of its function and ignorance will inevitably lead to disqualification. Even with older athletes I always point out to them that they are starting in the acceleration zone and that they must only pass the baton between the lines marking the take-over zone itself. This apart, the athlete is allowed to start from anywhere within the defined zone. I would stress the word "within" since athletes must not have even a foot over the line marking the beginning of the appropriate zone, i.e. the acceleration zone in the case of legs not exceeding 200 m, or the take-over zone in all other events. To do so means that the athlete is beginning the run from ouside the prescribed zone and is liable to disqualification.

Where the race is run entirely or partly in lanes, the Umpire must be satisfied that after passing the baton the incoming athlete does not in any way impede other athletes by crossing into their lane. Should this happen it is quite likely to result in the disqualification of the offending team. In addition, incoming athletes are not allowed to push-off their out-going partner.

A further problem for the Umpire occurs when a baton is dropped during an attempted take-over. Contrary to popular belief this does not automatically disqualify the team concerned, but the rules state that the baton must be picked up by the athlete who dropped it. This is in itself often a difficult decision for the official to make! The baton may be retrieved even though it may fall or roll outside the lane of the athletes concerned. If this can be achieved without impeding other athletes and if the eventual take-over occurs within the take-over zone of the team concerned, then the team may continue in the race without penalty. If the baton is dropped other than at a change-over the same facility is offered to the athlete concerned, even if the baton bounces on to the inside of the track. On retrieving the baton the athlete must regain the correct lane immediately so as not to reduce the distance run.

At the finish of the race an official should be designated to collect the batons from the athletes. The habit of throwing the baton into the air, in exhilaration or annoyance, after finishing the race constitutes a potential danger to other athletes, and following a couple of quite serious injuries caused by this thoughtlessness the domestic rules were amended to make it clear that if the baton is "dropped or thrown from the hand" the team concerned may be disqualified.

As far as team membership is concerned there have been recent changes to the BAF Rules which brings them into line with those of the IAAF. Once a relay team has started in a competition it is now permissible for two additional athletes to be used as substitutes in the composition of the team for subsequent rounds. Once an athlete has been replaced by a substitute, though, he or she may not return to the team. It is, of course, quite permissible for a team to run the same members but in a different order between heats and a subsequent round or final without having to notify anyone. It is, naturally, not allowed for one athlete to run two or more legs in any relay.

The Umpire has a number of tasks to undertake if officiating at a take-over where the event is being run in lanes. Firstly, there is the need to ensure that all of the teams contesting the race are represented at the change-over. Having ascertained that fact, then it is essential that the athletes are given their correct lane and notified of the location of the relevant zone markings and the significance of them. Once the athletes have placed their one check mark the official in charge will need to signal to the Starter (or Starter's Marksman) that all is in order. This is usually achieved following a blast on a whistle with the number of blasts corresponding to the number of the change-over. A clear signal by means of a white flag or disc will indicate to the Starter that the take-over is ready. Never be afraid to show a red signal if you are unhappy or uncertain about the lane draw. It is better for all concerned that any uncertainty is resolved before the race to avoid the possible need for a re-run.

Finally, the Umpires must decide where is the best place to stand in order to undertake the specific duties given to them. One guiding principle should be to stand well back from the edge of the track. On the whole, I would recommend a position on the inside of the track since from here there should be a clearer view of the teams. If a position is taken up on the outside, athletes in the outer lanes are likely to impede the view of those towards the inside. Once the batons have been exchanged the Umpire should make a clear signal to the official in charge indicating whether the takeovers were valid. That designated official should then use a white flag or disc to indicate that all is clear, or a red (or more often now yellow) signal to indicate an infringement, holding the signal aloft until an acknowledgement from the Referee has been received.

Relay races run in lanes provide their own crop of problems for the officials, but those in which lanes only operate for a section of the race produce another set of headaches. The most common race of this kind is the 4×400 m, the traditional closing event of many track and field meetings. It is customary to run either the first bend or the first three bends of the race in lanes with the break from lanes in both cases occurring at the standard break line for the 800 m. Since the staggers involved in running three bends in lanes are enormous it is only feasible to use this where the track has an adequate system of speakers to relay the instructions of the Starter. Where this is used the first change-over occurs in lanes between specially marked takeover zones, each 20 m in length. With the first bend only being run in lanes the athletes will have already moved to the inside of the track long before the first change-over is reached.

At the change-over when the athletes no longer run in lanes there is bound to be an element of confusion as the outgoing athletes jockey for position at the leading end of the take-over zone. It is usual to place the outgoing athletes at the commencement of the zone in the order in which they were drawn at the start. It is best if this is done from, say, lane 3 outwards leaving the inside of the track clear. My usual instruction then to the athletes is that they are free to take up a position on the inside of the track if their team is clearly in the lead. Inevitably there will be a certain amount of movement on the line if the race is still close and positions are changing as the incoming athletes approach the take-over. It is important for the Umpires to watch that teams are not impeded by others whilst in the act of passing the baton. Any obvious attempt to impede others intentionally should produce a disqualification for the team concerned.

Under recently introduced IAAF Rules (but not BAF Rules) the athletes are supposed to place themselves in their waiting position in the same order as their respective team members as they pass the 200 m point of the lap. Once the incoming athletes have passed this point the waiting runners are not allowed to change their positions, even though the race order may change drastically in the course of the second 200. It is likely that this will produce some major changes of direction as the incoming athletes approach the takeover and find their partners in inconvenient positions. Time will tell whether this produces more problems than it solves.

Relays provide great excitement for the spectators but also bring the largest number of disqualifications. Umpires should be particularly vigilant when undertaking any of the duties outlined here and must be quite positive that an infringement has taken place before making a report to the Referee.

The Wind Gauge

Amongst the duties which may be allocated to an Umpire is responsibility for recording wind speeds using a wind gauge. Although such a gauge may not be available on all tracks, the information is essential for any record claim for events of 200 m or less, as well as for the long and triple jumps. There are a number of types of gauge currently in use but most are of a broadly similar design and there are certain basic rules which govern their use. (See photograph on page 20).

Most gauges consist of a metal cylinder open at both ends, with a vane inside which rotates according to the strength and direc-

The official who is going to operate the gauge must be aware of several important procedures. The object of the gauge is to measure the average wind speed for the period for which the check is made. The period of time for which the wind component is measured varies, but is designed to cover roughly the length of time an athlete would be running if establishing a world record for the event.

The period for which the wind component should be measured in track races is as follows

All distances up to and including 100 m	10 seconds
100 m Hurdles and 110 m Hurdles	13 seconds
200 m commencing as the athletes enter the straight	10 seconds

The standard gauge has a switch which has three active positions marked 5 seconds (for long/triple jump), 10 seconds and 13 seconds. The switch is set against the time appropriate to the distance of the race. The gauge is operated by pressing a separate lever when the gun is fired (for events run wholly in the straight), or when the leading athlete enters the straight in a 200m race. There will either be a dial with a needle which will come to rest against a given figure at the end of the allotted time, or, more usually, a digital read-out to one or two decimal places.

It is vital that the wind speed is correctly identified as either following or against the direction of running. Unfortunately, it is not always apparent from the gauge since both the numbered dial and the digital read-out presuppose that the gauge is aligned in a certain direction, e.g. that a wind blowing from right to left is a following wind. There is always a clear indication on the gauge as to which direction is being read as plus (following) and which minus (against). If the gauge in use is not calibrated to show the correct reading for the given direction of

tion of the wind flowing through the cylinder. For track events the gauge should be set up 50 m from the finish line, along the straight, adjacent to lane 1. It is not always possible to site the gauge in exactly the correct position because of the location of the area used for presentations. The gauge should be erected no more than 2 m from the edge of the track "at a height of approximately 1.22 m". The latter extract from the rules (112.9) requires some clarification. It would be reasonable for an inexperienced official to ask which part of the gauge should be at the stated height since this is not identified within the rule. Bearing in mind that it is the vane which is rotating within the cylinder, the measurement should be taken to the centre spindle of the vane.

In setting up the gauge care should be taken to ensure that the cylinder is parallel to the edge of the track and perfectly horizontal. A simple spirit level will enable the latter to be checked easily and quickly.

running it can either be turned round (although this leaves the operator with back to the track) or a note can be fixed to the gauge to remind everyone that the directional component must be reversed.

In recording the wind speed from either type of gauge it should be noted that both domestic and IAAF Rules require the reading to be returned only to one decimal place of a metre per second. Where the digital read-out or information from the calibrated dial give speeds to two decimal places these must be rounded up to the next higher tenth of a metre per second in the positive direction. (For example, a reading of $+2.03$ m/s, must be recorded as $+2.1$ m/s; a reading of -2.03 m/s, must be recorded as -2.0 m/s).

It is important that the wind speed, particularly the direction, is checked before the gauge is re-set for the next race, and that the information is passed to the Referee or results steward so that the details can appear on the official result of the race. The Referee may well provide the officials operating the gauge with a recording slip which will then be filed with the rest of the details of the race. There are some n.c.r. pads now available commercially and it is useful to have a supply of these, or other duplicated slips, when acting as Referee where a gauge is likely to be in use. (See the example, Fig. 3 below).

The first two chapters have tried to outline the various duties you might be assigned as a Track Judge and/or Umpire. The repeated references to the role of the Track Referee underline the importance of this official to the smooth running of the meeting. In the next section consideration will be given to the specific duties which fall on that official's shoulders and will offer some advice as to how the task of refereeing might be approached.

WIND READING

	Date

Meeting	

		Wind Speed	
Event number		FOLLOWING **+**	AGAINST **—**
Event			
Heat No.	Semi-final No.	Final	

STACY REF. 154   Signature_____

Fig. 3. Wind Gauge Recording Form.

CHAPTER 3

ROLE AND DUTIES OF THE TRACK REFEREE

The principal duties of the track Referee under domestic rules are listed in Appendix E of the BAF Rulebook as follows:

(i) Have charge of all track events.
(ii) Allocate duties to Track Judges and Umpires.
(iii) Decide in the event of any difference of opinion between the Track Judges. The Referee's decision shall be final.
(iv) Deal with any disputed point as provided by the Rules.

The first of these duties is all-embracing but stresses the importance of the position. The Referee is directly or indirectly responsible for everything that happens on the track and must ensure that the Rules of Competition are observed at all times. There is also the obvious necessity to liaise with a number of different groups of officials who are contributing to the general organisation of the track events within the meeting. These will include the meeting organiser, the starters and marksmen, timekeepers, clerk of the course, announcer, seeders, results team and the many other officials who are involved in the quite complex organisation of even a small-scale athletics meeting.

The second is in many ways the most difficult and demanding on the Referee, and must require our particular attention here. As we have seen, whether judging or umpiring, there are a number of quite different duties which must be undertaken if there are sufficient officials available and it is up to you as Referee to allocate these duties. What should be the guiding principles in this allocation? First and foremost you must be certain there are sufficient judges on the stand to obtain as accurate a result as possible. There is little comfort in telling athletes and team managers after a race that you don't know what the result was but you are satisfied that no-one infringed any rules on the way! Secondly you must attempt to allocate the umpiring duties so that you can be reasonably certain that no rules have been infringed in the course of the event within the limitation of the number of officials who are available to you.

In many meetings you may well find that there are so few helpers that there is no possibility of allocating any umpiring duties at all. Under these circumstances your main consideration must be the accuracy of the result, although you should do your best to view the race from the top of the stand to identify any problems which might occur.

Where you have in advance the names of the officials who have accepted the invitation to the meeting and a copy of the timetable of events, the preparation of a worksheet is possible. Generally speaking it is usual for the Referee to allocate officials to both judging and umpiring duties in the course of the meeting, but there are some important considerations which should be borne in mind when producing the set of duties which may be summarised as follows:–

1. Ensure that your officials have a variety of activities to undertake in the course of the meeting.
2. Endeavour to give all your officials opportunities to judge sprint races, even though you are aware that some of them are inexperienced. It is only by working with more experienced colleagues that they will gain the confidence needed to progress.
3. Only ask your more experienced officials to judge the last 3 or 4 competitors in a sprint race. As has been said elsewhere, this is the most demanding of tasks and you must be able to rely on the result being offered by that official. It is unfair to ask a novice judge to attempt this, unless there are no others available.

4. Make certain that all of your judges gain a high position on the judges' stand some time in the course of the meeting.

5. Avoid giving your officials umpiring duties in consecutive events in widely dispersed locations on the track. There is nothing more annoying for an umpire than to be expected to get from one end of the track to the other in the, perhaps, short time between events.

6. Make sure that the person you appoint in charge of a take-over in a relay is a good organiser who will be able to deploy the rest of the team effectively and cope with possible problems with equanimity.

7. If you wish your officials to undertake any other specific duties in the course of the meeting, it is worthwhile including this on the instructions on the worksheet. (For example, you may wish them to assist the Clerk of the Course by removing hurdles from the track at the end of an event).

8. In a long meeting attempt to provide all of your team with a period away from judging and umpiring duties. This both allows the official to obtain refreshments and provides a short break from the high level of concentration which a busy meeting demands.

9. It is certainly advisable to appoint a Chief Judge from your team who will take your place if you are called from the stand for any reason. This must be someone you can trust to control the meeting in your temporary absence. This official should not be given any other specific duties on your worksheet.

10. If you have sufficient time when compiling your worksheet, it is useful to look at your allocation of duties and plan ahead in case one (or more) of your judges fails to arrive without warning. This may not become apparent until the meeting is just about to start, but you need to be alert to what duties you have allocated to any missing official and re-arrange your list of duties where necessary. It is often difficult to find

time once the meeting has begun, so a little prior thought may pay dividends on the day.

There are various ways of compiling your worksheet but an example is included for reference on page 24. On this worksheet the numbers refer to the umpiring positions shown on the map on page 9. As can be seen, the meeting was fairly well-staffed with officials and each person had a variety of activities to undertake.

Deciding the result of the race

Under domestic rules one of the main tasks of the Referee is to decide what is the official result of a race. At the end of the race the judges should display their boards to the Referee who will normally be located at the top of the judges' stand during the race. If the judges are all agreed, then the task of the Referee is simply to transfer that verdict on to the result pad, whether personally in agreement with that result or not. With longer distance races it is more efficient to ask one of the judges to call out carefully what he or she has recorded whilst the remainder check this against their result. Any variations can be identified once the judge has completed calling the full result.

In some races, especially where there have been eight runners in a sprint race, there may well not be unanimity amongst the judges, and the Referee must decide what the final result will be. It is usually quite easy to resolve this problem by using a majority basis, i.e. if the majority of the judges have athlete No. 3 in a given position ahead of athlete No. 4, then No. 3 can be given the higher place. The wording of this particular function of the Referee, namely to "decide in the case of a difference of opinion between the track judges", is open to a number of interpretations. On the whole, most Referees do not bring their own result into consideration unless the judges are evenly split in their decision. In some cases, though, the

BRITISH ATHLETICS LEAGUE   DIVISION 5   5th JUNE 1993

TRACK JUDGING AND UMPIRING SCHEDULE

Chief Judge : JL	DH	WT	JG	BW	HG	GR	MT
2.30 400m Hurdles	J	J	11	13	17	21	J
2.45 800m	BR	11/6	LBB	J	J	J	19
3.00 100m	J	J	WG	J	5	7	JL3
3.15 3000m S/C	H3	H2	LS	H4	LS	LBB	WJ
3.30 110m Hurdles	J	7	JL3	WG	J	5	J
3.45 400m	17	J	J	J	11/6	J	22
4.00 1500m	J	19	11	15	LBB	J	J
4.15 200m	JL3	J	J	J	19	22	WG
4.30 5000m	19	11	LS	LS	LS	LS	LBB
5.00 4x100m	IC2	J	11/J	IC3	TO2	TO1	IC1
5.25 4x400m	TOi	TOi	TOo	19	BR	11	J*

LBB Lap board and bell. Official to judge as well.

11/6 Cover 11 but move to 6 for end of race. Similarly 11/J.

BR   Cover Break and remain at 14 for remainder of race.

J Judge all places	**JL3** Judge last three places
LS Lap score	**WG** Wind gauge
H Steeplechase hurdle	**WJ** Water jump
IC In charge of the take-over	**C of C** to judge in 4×100
TOi Take over in & Judge	**TOo** Take over out then to 6

J*   To watch specifically for obstruction at the takeovers

4 x 400 Relay will be run from short staggers (i.e. 130m only in lanes)

Fig. 4. Judges' Worksheet.

Referee may wish to give preference to the results recorded by those located well up on the stand who have a better view of the finish, and similarly preference may well be given to the result of the judge who had a particular duty to record only the last three or four athletes when deciding these places, and this seems quite acceptable. It is essential that the Referee informs the judges what result is being given. Judges should check this result against their own board to ensure that an incorrect number is not being called.

It should be noted that under recently introduced IAAF Rules the role of the Track Referee at this level is somewhat different, since the Chief Judge is given the task of allocating duties to the judges. (IAAF Rule 118.1) This simply means that the procedures mentioned in the earlier paragraphs would be undertaken by that official rather than the Track Referee. It is something of an anomaly that the Referee under IAAF Rules remains the person who allocates duties to umpires. (IAAF Rule 119.2). In Great Britain at most international meetings the officials appointed would be expected to act as both judges and umpires in the course of the meeting, and to have two different Chief Officials allocating duties to them seems unnecessarily complicated and this system is not usually adopted.

Dealing with infringements

The most difficult of the tasks facing the Referee of a meeting at any level is that of deciding whether to disqualify an athlete or team from the competition. As has been seen earlier there are a number of infringements which could bring disqualification, although under domestic rules the final decision usually rests with the Referee. Let us review the main areas of likely infringement and the possible actions which can be taken.

Advertising and clothing

Rule 17 deals with the vexed question of clothing and involves a number of possible problems.

(a) The basic rule states that "competitors must wear at least vest and shorts (or equivalent clothing) which are clean and so designed and worn as not to be objectionable, even if wet". The wording of the rule allows for the wearing of clothing which does not consist of the vest and shorts worn separately, but the decision of what constitutes clothing which is objectionable is a purely subjective one. This is a problem which should be dealt with at the assembly point for the athletes, or at the start. It is clearly a difficult decision for the Referee to take to disqualify an athlete after the race has been run. It is important that any concern about the suitability of the clothing is notified to that athlete rather than just be allowed to pass, even if no further action is to be taken.

(b) The second area of possible conflict occurs over the wearing of Club vests by athletes competing in a team or relay competition. The Rules (17.2) state quite clearly that "competitors shall wear the registered vest of the team they are representing, unless the Referee has given permission for a change to be made". Such permission will normally be requested in advance and often hinges on the non-availability of vests of a certain size or a delay in their production. The Referee must use discretion again in deciding whether such a claim appears valid. An added complication arises where a Club has more than one set of colours officially registered; in these circumstances either vest would be acceptable under the rule, but a Note does indicate that "in team or relay races all competitors should wear registered vests of the same design". (Note the use of the word "should" rather than "shall" in this rule, which stresses that this is a recommended rather than a compulsory requirement).

(c) "In individual County, District, Regional or National Championships athletes must wear the vest of their BAF affiliated Club or their County, Regional or National vest". (Note that once again the Referee is given the opportunity to grant permission for an alternative to be worn, but this should not be given retrospectively). The use of the word "must" in this rule makes this a compulsory requirement and renders any athlete infringing liable to disqualification.

(d) The question of advertising on vests is extremely complicated in some respects but is one of the major areas of conflict with athletes. Rule 16 is quite specific. If an affiliated Club has a sponsor it is permissible for the name of that sponsor to be worn provided that:

(i) the specific design of the advertising material has been approved and registered with the Federation.
(ii) the advertising appears only on the vest and/or tracksuit of the Club or Association concerned. (It is not permitted for an athlete of an officially sponsored Club to wear any sponsor identification on an alternative vest).
(iii) only one such advertisement, which must not exceed 3cm × 15cm in size, may appear on each vest or tracksuit, and this must be positioned off-centre on the vest, either to left or right. (Note that the exact measurements allowed are subject to amendment and should be checked carefully against the latest Rulebook).

Details of those Clubs which have officially approved sponsors can be obtained from the Federation Office in Birmingham.

(e) Apart from these sponsor identifications, athletes "are not allowed to take into the arena or course any form of advertising material, nor to display on their person any such advertising, other than:

(i) the accepted name of their affiliated Club in lettering which should not exceed 4cm in height.
(ii) a single Trade Mark of the manufacturer or supplier of the clothing they are wearing which must not exceed 20 square cm with a maximum height of 4cm". (Again, this is subject to amendment).

Unfortunately, many clothing manufacturers sell vests and shorts which contain advertising well in excess of these limits. In some cases the offending wording or logo may be covered by adhesive tape by the Starter's Marksmen before the athlete competes, but if allowed to start the Referee must decide what action to take. Certainly with young athletes I would plead for tolerance, but it is still very important that they are informed about the rules and in what way their kit does not conform.

Contrary to what one sometimes sees on television, under IAAF Rules the situation is very similar. In Championships and matches between countries athletes must wear the uniform clothing approved by their National Association. In all other meetings, including Grand Prix and other invitation meetings, athletes "shall participate in national uniform clothing or in club clothing officially approved by their National Governing Body". (IAAF Rule 139.1) It should also be noted that under this rule the Victory Ceremony and any lap of honour are considered to be part of the competition and the above clothing restrictions apply.

Footwear (Rule 102)

Far fewer problems are likely to be faced by the Referee over the question of footwear.

These rules have been much simplified in recent years and can be summarised:–

(i) Athletes may compete in bare feet if they wish, but if they compete in shoes they must not contain any kind of spring or device which gives any form of assistance.

(ii) The sole and heel of the shoes may be constructed to provide for the use of up to 11 spikes, although the athlete does not have to make use of all of the spike positions available.

(iii) For competitions on synthetic surfaces the part of the spike which projects from the sole or heel must not exceed 9mm for track events, with a maximum diameter of 4mm. On some tracks there may be an insistence on a smaller spike length at the discretion of the stadium management. On non-synthetic surfaces the maximum spike length is 25mm with the same maximum diameter of 4mm.

(iv) The sole and/or heel may have grooves, ridges, indentations and protuberances provided these features are constructed of the same or similar material to the basic sole itself.

(v) The sole of the shoe may be of any thickness.

Numbers (Rules 18 and 103)

This is another area of possible conflict between athletes and the Referee. The most important requirement is that "no competitor shall be allowed to take part in any competition without wearing the appropriate number cards and such cards must not be cut, folded or otherwise concealed in any way". (Rule 18.1) It is to be hoped that you do not come across athletes whose arrogance is such that they proclaim "I don't wear numbers. Everyone knows who I am!" which was reported to have been said by one world famous athlete.

It is important for all concerned that athletes wear the correct number and that it is clearly visible to the judges and the umpires on the one hand, and the spectators on the other. To allow some athletes to cut down their numbers can also be considered unfair to the remainder of the field, particularly on very hot days when there is a natural desire to allow as much ventilation to the body as possible, a feature which is unfortunately hampered by the presence of a large number card.

Under normal circumstances it is hoped that all track athletes will be provided with number cards to be worn on both breast and back. Prior consultation by the Referee with the Starter's Marksmen is useful in reminding these officials that there must be an insistence that the front number card is worn on the breast. Judges will readily confirm that life is made considerably easier at the finish if all of the approaching numbers are at a uniform level, notwithstanding the varying heights of the athletes themselves. Where photofinish is in operation, athletes will probably be required to wear adhesive numbers on the side of the shorts (or the bare leg) facing the camera or cameras.

Where the meeting or league has a sponsor, then the name of that sponsor may well be included on the number card. If this happens the lettering of the sponsor's name must not exceed 4cm in height and 15cm in width, or 48 square cm in total area. The name of the sponsor may appear either above or below the number itself. It is unfortunate that in some cases the advertising is given preference when the card is designed and the actual height of the digits of the number becomes quite small, making the task of the judge (and the umpire) much more difficult.

In many respects the IAAF Rules relating to number cards are more specific than those in the domestic rules. The International Rules stipulate that the maximum size of the card shall be 24cm by 20cm, and that the maximum height of the numerals shall not be less than 6cm nor more than 10cm in height. The maximum height of the sponsor's identification on the cards under these rules is 5cm. if the writing is above the numeral, and no more than 3cm if it is placed below. It is permitted for there to be two different sponsors for a given competition but the name of only one of them may appear on any single number card, and this must be common to all the cards used for a given race or field event.

Hopefully, any problems over clothing, footwear or numbers will have been resolved long before the athletes reach the track, by the officials in assembly or at the start by the Starter's Marksmen. In all cases of infringements in these areas the athlete concerned should be spoken to, even if no disciplinary action is to be taken by the Referee. Where possible the reason for the rule should be explained to the athlete at the same time.

Assistance (Rules 21 & 105)

This has been an area of contention for some time at both domestic and international level. The recent change of wording has hopefully clarified which particular type of possible assistance is covered by the restrictions here. "No competitor shall receive any advice or similar assistance during the progress of an event. 'Assistance' means direct help conveyed by any means including any technical device". There is an obvious difference between someone shouting "Come on" or similar encouragement and another calling "You are 10 metres clear and going away from the field". It will be up to the Referee to decide whether such information constitutes assistance within the spirit of the rule. One obvious problem is that the reporting Umpire may well be able to identify the person offering the advice but may not be clear which athlete the information was directed at.

Under IAAF Rules a recent change has produced considerable disquiet, particularly amongst athletes. The addition to Rule 143.2 states ". . no competitor shall **give or** receive assistance during the progress of an event". This is more likely to be a major problem in field events, especially Combined Events, where it is quite usual to see athletes conversing with each other in the course of the competition, often discussing each other's previous throw or jump. The addition to the rule may also have some implications for track events.

Pacemaking was for some time regarded as being included within the definition of "assistance", but has now been accepted, partly because in many instances the pacemaker was acting on behalf of all of the athletes in the race, whether they were aware of it or not, and therefore the only option was to disqualify the whole field for receiving assistance, even if unwittingly, or to disqualify the winner as being the athlete who had benefitted most from the pacemaking. The rule, however, does make mention of "pacemaking" stating that "assistance" is also to be interpreted as including pacing by persons not participating in the race. (The corresponding IAAF Rule 143.2 also includes within the definition of "assistance" pacing by athletes lapped or about to be lapped).

Another recent change has brought the domestic rules into line with those of the IAAF as far as "assistance" is concerned. It is now accepted that an infringement only occurs if the advice or similar assistance is given "from within the competition area". The problem of defining the "competition area" arises, and this will tend to vary from one track to another. If the outer edge of the track is bounded by a fence or wall then the competition area for track events is clearly anywhere within this boundary. Where there is no retaining barrier the boundary will have to be accepted as the outer edge of the track surface.

The final paragraph in this rule underlines

that "athletes receiving assistance as defined are liable to be disqualified". It is, of course, up to the discretion of the Referee whether such action will be taken.

The placing of Umpires

Certain general principles concerning the production of a worksheet by the Referee were dealt with above (page 22). With these in mind it is probably of some value to comment on the allocation of umpiring duties for specific events where the Referee has a reasonable number of officials to deploy.

For flat races run entirely on the straight, Umpires placed beyond the finish line (Positions 5-8 on the umpiring map) will provide adequate coverage to identify impedance of one athlete by another. If the Referee has a large number of officials available, a second team placed beyond the start line (Positions 1-4) will provide additional support for any reported infringement. It is obviously not necessary to utilise all of the umpiring positions at these points.

A similar pattern can be adopted for hurdle races run entirely on the straight. In these cases the Umpires viewing the athletes on the very inside and outside of the field should be aware that they are looking for possible trailing of the leg or foot below the plane of the top of the bar, in addition to the other possible infringements. It is valuable to place an Umpire(s) at position 37 and/or 24 to watch specifically for the taking down of the hurdle deliberately with the hand or foot. In circumstances where there is an abundance of officials a similar role could be given to Umpires at positions 36 and 38 or their outside track equivalents. It must be stressed that most infringements in hurdles events can best be seen from a head-on position.

For events run wholly or partly in lanes around the bend, the Referee must attempt to provide as much umpiring cover as

possible to ensure that athletes do not run on or over their lane lines. Positions 13 and 17 are particularly valuable to use since the Umpire concerned may watch not only part of the bend but also the progress of the athletes along the back straight. The coverage provided will obviously be dependent on the number of officials available. With limited resources, positions 11 and 19 will provide reasonable coverage of the bends but it is obviously better to have more umpires deployed if possible. It is worthwhile remembering that lane running in the home straight also needs to be observed either from the Judges' stand, or, ideally, by an Umpire or Umpires located at some of positions 5-8.

With the 300m and 400m hurdle events there is a need for the Umpire to watch both possible lane infringements and faulty hurdle clearances and this is a difficult task. Where possible, the Referee should aim to have one Umpire to each flight of hurdles, with another two at positions 11 and 19 to watch specifically for lane running infringements. The Umpires should be left to find the best vantage point to observe their particular flight of hurdles, but it should be stressed that a position well in advance of the hurdle on the outside lane is essential if the task is to be satisfactorily accomplished and all eight hurdles observed. Once the athletes have cleared the hurdle for which the Umpire is directly responsible they should be observed by that official for as long as a clear view is obtained. In the case of a report of a faulty clearance it is obviously advantageous if more than one report is received by the Referee on the same incident.

Lane running infringements take on an even greater importance if the meeting is being held under IAAF Rules since the mandatory disqualification for running on or over the inside lane line on the bend applies, and this is true for both flat races and those held over hurdles.

With Steeplechase events the Referee should attempt to place an official at each of the hurdles as well as at the water jump. The latter official will have the additional responsibility of ensuring that requisite sections of kerbing have been removed to allow access to an inside water jump, and that they are carefully replaced afterwards. Similarly, where the water jump is located on the outside of the track the Umpire should check that the cones, or other markers used to indicate the course, are correctly placed and removed after the race is completed. The photograph below shows the kind of view which an Umpire at a hurdle needs to have in order to identify possible infringements. On the whole I favour a position on the outside of the track rather than the inside, since many of the problems approaching a hurdle are caused by athletes moving to the outside of the field in order to have a clear view of the barrier, often obstructing other competitors in the process.

Where a break from lanes is to take place (i.e. in the 800m or 4 × 400m or other longer relay races) an Umpire must be placed to observe that the athletes do not break from their lane before the line. This break line should be identified by a flag or flags as a guide to the athletes. The Umpire should be placed at position 14 and reminded that this is the best position from which to view the break line. Under no circumstances should the Umpire be allowed to take up a position on the break line itself since this provides an inadequate view of possible infringements. The Referee should remember to acknowledge the signal from the Umpire at the

Note that the leg of the barrier should be flush with the kerbing.

Break before concentrating on following the runners around the track.

Relay Races

The relay event run in lanes requires a careful allocation of available officials to the various duties. Remembering the basic need to ensure the accuracy of the result from the judges left on the stand, Umpires in a 4 × 100m race should be allocated to take-overs on a disproportional basis. The first exchange is the most difficult to judge since the spread of the athletes around the track is greatest at this point and, in ideal circumstances, demands the use of at least one more official than at the other change-overs. The second change is only marginally easier and should be as well staffed as possible. The end of the zone of the final change usually occurs on a virtual straight line and therefore this constitutes the least demanding change as far as officials are concerned.

The Referee may wish to allocate particular duties to the officials at the change-overs, but it is usual to nominate someone to be in charge and allow them to position the available officials. In allocating teams to change-overs it is important for the Referee to remember that both the acceleration zone and the end of the take-over zone need to be closely observed, especially if all of the track lanes are in use. As with other events run around the bend, the Referee should aim to have at least one Umpire on each bend to ensure fair running. Sadly, at many meetings, the extent of the coverage available will be minimal and the Referee must decide which are the vital duties to be undertaken with these limited resources.

For relays in which lanes are only used for part of the race, care should be taken to ensure that the section of the race run in lanes is well staffed with Umpires, even if some are requested to return to the stand once lanes have ceased to operate. The break line needs to be manned as do the front and end of the take-over zones. It is advisable for the Referee to appoint an Umpire to watch for possible impedance during the act of passing the baton. The Referee should normally oversee the race, especially the change-overs, from a high position on the judges' stand.

Qualification for subsequent rounds

In an event where heats are to be run a system for deciding which athletes progress forward will have been decided in advance. If the qualifying conditions are, say, that the first two in each heat progress to the final there is seldom any problem unless the Referee declares a dead-heat for second place in one of the heats. Quite frequently, though, the qualification is made on a combination of places and times. The rules state that in preliminary rounds at least the winner, and preferably the winner and second, should qualify for the next round or final. After that qualifying places may be allocated according to times.

In a 200m event, for example, the qualification might well be the first two in each of three heats and the two fastest losers passing to the final. In the case of the fastest losers there may be three or more athletes with identical times but only two lanes available in the final. Quite understandably Chief Timekeepers should not allow qualification to be based on times recorded manually to one hundredth of a second, even though their colleagues will have recorded such times from their watches. Whilst the standard of timekeeping in this country is the highest in the world, it is impossible to be consistently accurate to within one hundredth of a second. If it is not possible to resolve the problem by bringing into use an extra lane, then the athletes tying must be asked to compete again against each other to decide who is going to occupy the remaining place(s) in the next round.

Where this situation occurs the Referee must ensure that the minimum rest period between the last heat of one round and the re-run is allowed, and that a similar minimum period is allowed between the re-run and the following round or final.

This may require that the timetable is modified and careful liaison must be carried out between the Referee and all other interested parties. In producing the timetable for the English Schools' Championships over many years I made it a practice to identify slots for re-runs of all sprint races, and especially hurdle races. These were known to the Meeting Manager, so when there was a need to initiate a qualifying race this could be put in place with a minimum of delay and discussion.

Under domestic rules the minimum rest periods between the start of the last heat in a round and the first heat of the subsequent round or final are:—

	Minimum rest (minutes)
Up to and including 100 m	20
Over 100 m and up to 200 m	40
Over 200 m and up to 400 m	60
Over 400 m and up to 800 m	80
Over 800 m	100

(One of the first duties of the Referee is to scrutinise the timetable on receipt to ensure that at least the minimum rests are provided in any competition where heats are being contested).

Under IAAF rules the time allocations are much greater, but it should be remembered that these rules will be largely applied at major Championships lasting several days.

The times recommended, where practicable, are:—

	Minimum rest (minutes)
Up to and including 200 m	45
Over 200 m and up to and including 1000 m	90
Over 1000 m	Not on the same day

In confirming the athletes who are to contest any re-run the Referee should be careful not to include ineligible athletes, even though with similar times. To give an example, if the qualification in a series of semi-finals is for the first three and two fastest losers to progress to the final and the result of the semi-finals of the 100 m is:—

	Race 1	
1.	14	10.8 s
2.	25	10.9 s
3.	54	10.9 s
4.	3	11.0 s
5.	18	11.0 s
6.	10	11.1 s
Wind speed +3.2 m/s		

	Race 2	
1.	23	10.7 s
2.	1	10.8 s
3.	7	10.8 s
4.	5	10.9 s
5.	17	11.0 s
6.	19	11.1 s
Wind speed +1.5 m/s		

who would be the qualifiers?

After removing the first three athletes in each race as automatic qualifiers, and competitor no. 5 as an obvious qualifier on time, we are left with three athletes with identical times (11.0 s) but only one place in the final remaining. In these circumstances the Referee will need to organise a run-off but should only ask competitors nos. 3 and 17 to take part. As there is only one place remaining to be filled competitor no. 18, having already been beaten by no. 3, can make no claim to be considered. (See page 42 for the situation regarding fastest losers when photofinish is in operation).

The Referee should be aware that decisions may be taken by the seeders or recorders without consultation, spuriously based on positions in the race (e.g. they could give the place to no. 3 purely on the basis of the athlete's place in the race relative to the other possible fastest loser) or even on the respective wind speeds (e.g. no. 17 might be given the place because aided by a less favourable following wind). Neither of these is acceptable as a means of deciding qualifiers. It is important that the Referee or the Track Steward, where appointed, keeps a check on the fastest losers to ensure that the correct athletes progress to the next round or are invited to re-run for the available place(s).

In the case of a dead-heat for first place in the final of an event the Referee has the option of asking the athletes concerned to compete again to decide the winner. Although this is provided for in the rules I have yet to hear of a Track Referee invoking it.

Disqualifications

When the Referee has taken the decision to disqualify an athlete it is important that this information is passed to the athlete concerned as quickly as possible. It is most unfortunate if the first notice athletes have of their disqualification is to hear it over the public address system.

It is the duty of the Referee to explain carefully to the athlete the reasons for the disqualification. Under IAAF rules the Umpire(s) must have produced a written report for the Referee which can be most useful in identifying both the exact nature of the infringement and where it is claimed to have happened. Over the years I have used an infringement slip modified from one first produced for the 1986 Commonwealth Games in Edinburgh and this is currently in general use in the country. A copy of this slip is shown on page 34. Whilst mandatory for meetings under IAAF rules, it is also very useful for any meeting where Umpires are deployed around the track.

Protests

Under domestic rules (Rules 23 & 106) there are two quite different types of protest which can be made and the procedures for dealing with them differ accordingly.

The first of these concerns "protests or objections by a competitor or a team against the conduct or placing of another competitor or team in any competition or relating to any matter which may develop during the carrying-out of the programme". The latter would include protests about the disqualification of an athlete. The protest must be made "immediately after the competition", verbally, by the individual competitor or by a member of the protesting Club. The Referee then decides any protest or objection and that decision is final in all circumstances.

The second type of protest is one against the eligibility of an athlete or a team to compete in a given competition. This protest may be made in advance of the competition, but where this has not been possible the protest is made to the Referee. Where such a protest occurs on the day the details must be set down in writing and signed by the individual objector, by a member of the protesting team, or by the Secretary of the protesting Club, and accompanied by a deposit of £10. The Referee may decide the protest on the spot, but if this is objected to at the time the

EVENT: ....   UMPIRING POSITION No. ....

Heat No. ....   UMPIRE No. ....

Semi-final No. ....

Final   (signature)

DETAILS OF INFRINGEMENT / INCIDENT

Comp. No.

Ran on or over lane line (....... strides .... cms out of lane)

Broke ...... metres before Break Line

Stepped off the track for .... strides on lap No. ......

Impeded Competitor No. .... (Details below)

Trailed leg around hurdle, flight No. ....

Knocked down hurdle deliberately, flight No. ....

Trailed leg around steeplechase barrier No. .... on lap No. ....

Failed to clear water jump correctly on lap No. ....

Received assistance or coaching - details below

Retired from race on lap No. ....

Other infringement/incident or additional information - details overleaf.

PLEASE INDICATE ON TRACK PLAN EXACT POSITION OF INFRINGEMENT/INCIDENT

Fig. 5. Infringement Slip.

matter has to be referred to the relevant Regional or National Association of the BAF. Any prizes likely to be affected by the result of the protest must be withheld until the matter is finally resolved.

Under IAAF Rules (Rule 147) protests about eligibility must be made to the Jury of Appeal, or, if no Jury has been appointed, to the Referee before the meeting begins. If the matter cannot be satisfactorily resolved prior to the meeting, the athlete concerned is allowed to compete "under protest" and the matter referred to the IAAF Council.

A protest under IAAF Rules concerning the result or the conduct of an event must be made verbally to the Referee by the athlete or a representative of that athlete. The Referee may be able to take the opportunity of viewing a film or picture provided by an official video tape recorder. (This is likely to be a video produced by the company televising the meeting, although it could be argued that this is not "official" unless previously designated as such). The Referee may either decide the protest at this point, or refer it to the Jury of Appeal. If the Referee takes a decision the athlete has a right of appeal to the Jury. When this happens the Referee is likely to be asked for all of the relevant documentation, including umpiring slips, and may be called before the Jury to justify the decision made. The Jury then decides the protest. The Jury usually provides the Referee with a written report of its finding before the decision is made public.

So much for the occasionally demanding duties of the Track Referee! In the following sections reference will be made to the specific responsibilities of the Track Clerk of the Course, and the action required of track officials when a National Record is established and needs documentation. There is also a section giving a brief introduction to the use of photofinish at major meetings, and a final chapter provides details of the current grading system for technical officials operative in the United Kingdom.

CHAPTER 4

DUTIES OF THE CLERK OF THE COURSE (TRACK)

In the organisation of a successful athletics meeting on the track the importance of the role of the Clerk of the Course cannot be over-emphasised. It is strongly recommended that at all but the simplest track meeting an experienced official is specifically appointed to this position.

The tasks to be undertaken by the Clerk of the Course will vary according to the complexity of the meeting and the nature of the programme of events, but the following "check list" may be useful as a guide.

Prior to the Start of the Meeting (where appropriate)

(1) Become familiar with all of the standard track markings, especially relevant start lines and hurdle positions.

(2) Ensure that the judges' and timekeepers' stands and finish posts are in position. Where possible, isolate judging and timekeeping areas by means of ropes or other barriers to avoid the view of the officials being obstructed by over-enthusiastic spectators and athletes.

(3) Ensure that the lap board and bell are in position at the finish and in working order.

(4) Ensure that the starter's rostrum/stand is available for the Chief Starter.

(5) Check telephone links from track-side to the announcer and/or photofinish.

(6) Install the wind gauge in its correct location and at the right height, and check that it is operational. (See page 19).

(7) Provide appropriate signal flag for Chief Timekeeper, if required.

(8) Ensure that flags indicating the position of the Break Line in the 800 m/4 × 400 m Relay are in place and visible.

(9) Provide signal flags for the official at the Break Line, either in proximity to the line itself or at the judges' stand, as required by the Track Referee.

(10) Locate flags at 1 km points in any steeplechase event, if required by the Chief Timekeeper.

(11) Clearly mark by flags or posts significant intermediate points in races (e.g. 1500 m in a 1 mile race), if this is requested by the Track Referee.

(12) Check each steeplechase barrier to ensure it is safe to use.

(13) Cone sections of bends without kerbing whenever possible. (Liaise also with appropriate field event officials about the removal and eventual replacement of kerbing during high jump/javelin competitions).

During the Meeting

(1) Ensure that the track is kept clear at all times.

(2) Ensure that sets of starting blocks are in position at appropriate start lines.

(3) Ensure at the appropriate time that hurdles are placed on their correct marks and at the correct height and toppling weight. (See page 13). Liaise with the Track Referee as to the possibility/desirability of placing some lanes of hurdles on the track during a preceding race or races. It may be necessary to arrange for a signal to be given to the starter/marksmen to indicate that the hurdles are all in place. This is particularly useful in the case of 300 m and 400 m hurdle events. Whenever possible arrange for the hurdle flights nearest to the start to be put in place first, since this allows athletes additional time to check their run up to the first few hurdles.

(4) Arrange for the hurdles to be cleared from the track as quickly as possible and indicate to the starter/marksmen when this has been achieved.

(5) Arrange for the water jump to be filled well in advance of the timetabled start of the event and have the water level topped-up, if necessary, just prior to the race.

(6) Arrange for the steeplechase barriers to be placed on the appropriate marks and at the correct stage of the race. (See page 16). Particular care should be taken to ensure that the barrier is placed so that the front of the bar facing the athletes as they approach is marked in contrasting colours to assist in sighting, and that the foot of the hurdle is in contact with the edge of the kerbing. (See photograph page 30).

(7) Arrange for any section of kerbing to be removed to give the athletes access to, and exit from, the water jump. Where the water jump is placed on the outside of the track, arrange for appropriate coning of the track leading to and from the jump.

(8) Ensure that barriers and cones are removed from the track, and kerbing replaced, as soon as the steeplechase event is over.

(9) Liaise with appropriate field event officials about the removal and eventual replacement of track kerbing during high jump/javelin competitions.

(10) Provide batons at the judges stand when relays are included in the programme. (Note that it is often better to arrange for the batons to be made available only a short time before the relay events to avoid possible removal by practising teams!).

(11) Arrange for sets of flags or discs for each take-over position to be available at the judges' stand.

Following the Meeting

(1) Return batons, lap board, bell, flags, starting blocks and any other equipment to the central store or equipment room.

(2) Dismantle the wind gauge and return to the central store. (This may be conveniently undertaken as soon as the last sprint race has been run).

The Clerk of the Course will need to have available a tape measure to check heights of hurdles. In addition, where appropriate, a spring balance (to test hurdle toppling weights) and a spirit level (to assist in the accurate setting-up of the wind gauge) would be useful. A readily available copy of the current Rulebook is essential.

CHAPTER 5

PHOTOFINISH

Whilst most track judges are not expected to be in any way conversant with the operation of photofinish in track races, it is expected that those aspiring to become Grade 1 should have some awareness of the principles involved. Hopefully, though, what follows may prove of general interest to all track judges, qualified or not.

Photofinish is not a new development in the sport. Judges in the 1932 Olympic Games in Los Angeles viewed a film of the 100 metres Mens' Final to decide the result. The inventor of the camera used on that occasion, G. T. Kirby, was able to state after the event "The seven judges and myself have viewed the film of the finish several times. We can state that Tolan won by exactly five hundredths of a second." Interestingly, under present rules the race would have been awarded on this evidence to the runner-up, Ralph Metcalfe, who reached the line ahead of his rival, but the then rule stated that the athlete's torso had to be completely beyond the finish line, a fact proved by the camera and giving Eddie Tolan the gold medal. This rule was changed in 1933, no doubt partly in response to the result of this race. From that date to the present time the torso has only to reach the edge of the finish line to complete the race.

In recent years there have been dramatic developments in the technology of photofinish and now at least six different systems may be encountered within the country and that number seems destined to rise still further. It is not necessary to deal with all six of these in any detail but three distinct systems require specific explanation.

The object of photofinish, irrespective of the system used, is to produce an image on film or on a monitor which will identify the finishing order of a race and enable the time of each of the competitors to be read to a high degree of accuracy. For a long time the means of achieving this was by recording the finish on film, as was the case with the 1932 Olympic race, but the latest developments use sophisticated video cameras and allow the images to be recorded either onto tape or optical discs for later retrieval.

It is perhaps possible to grasp the principle of photofinish if we begin with one of these new video-based systems. In this relatively simple system the video camera is carefully aligned so that a vertical cursor line runs directly down the nearer edge of the finish line i.e. the plane marking the end of the race. (See page 1). A timing device within the system is activated by the start signal and the changing time is displayed on the screen, as it is during many transmissions of sporting events on television. As athletes approach the finish line the images from the camera can be recorded onto a video cassette. Using a modified video recorder the tape may then be replayed and "frozen" as each athlete reaches the edge of the finish line marked by the vertical cursor. The time of each athlete's arrival at the line is visible from the display on the screen and the result can be compiled. The video camera has acted very much as the eye of a judge on the finish line would have done, seeing the athlete both for a short distance in advance of the line and a little beyond it too.

The disadvantage of most of the systems using this technique is that the screen image is replaced or "scanned" only 50 times a second, so that successive images produced represent the position at the finish line 1/50th second apart. Some athletes not quite reaching the edge of the finish line on one screen may well be past it on the next, 1/50th second later. This presents no problem with times since the longer one would be recorded, but does so if the relative position of athletes changes between the first and second screen. Since the positions as they actually reached the plane of the finish can only be guessed the one option open to the

Chief Photofinish Judge is to declare a dead-heat between the athletes concerned. (IAAF Rule 121.5).

For a long time photofinish cameras using film to record the images seen through the lens have overcome the problem of recording every athlete actually reaching the plane of the finish. Unlike the previously mentioned video camera the image falling onto the film does not show the area in front of and beyond the finish line. Although the lens is exactly the same as would be used with an ordinary 35 mm camera, a metal plate or other barrier is placed between the lens and the film. The plate or barrier has only a very small slit in it a fraction of a millimetre wide and this is carefully aligned so that it runs exactly along the leading edge of the finish line.

Unlike a standard 35 mm camera, where a shutter opens and closes to record the scene at a given moment of time, or a cine camera where a number of separate frames are recorded each second, the normal photofinish camera, when activated, runs a continuous piece of film across the slit, recording everything which appears in that narrow gap in the plate. If the athlete's hand reaches the line first this will appear first on the film, followed by the rest of the body in turn. If the foot lands exactly on the finishing line this will appear in the slit for a comparatively long period of time producing an image on the moving film which suggests that the athlete has suddenly donned a ski!

As before, a timing device is activated by the start signal, and the elapsed time is imprinted on the bottom of the film as it moves across the slit by light emitting diodes. These cameras have a developing tank attached and once the exposed film has been passed through the developer and the fixer (to arrest further developing), and carefully washed in water to remove any remaining chemicals, it is ready to be placed in a viewer which will magnify the negative and enable

the result and times to be accurately read by means of a vertical cursor line. Each race can be separately identified by means of a "sequence number" which is recorded onto the base of the negative, below the timing marks, and is adjusted after each finish. This means of identification is essential if a particular race needs to be quickly located following a query about the result, or if it is established that a record performance has been achieved and a photograph is needed to support the claim.

A simpler type of camera became popular several years ago and incorporated the "slit" principle but produced the result in the form of a Polaroid photograph. This system is quite simple to set-up and does not require chemicals to process the film. Unfortunately, the resulting Polaroid photograph is limited in size and will only cover something like 2 seconds of exposure. This is quite suitable if a sprint race is being recorded but is of limited use when it comes to a middle distance race with a reasonable sized field. In order to record as much detail as possible on the limited amount of space available a beam is usually set up about a metre before the finish line and an athlete passing through this beam will trigger the shutter to open and then stop the exposure until the beam is broken again. A further problem of this system is that the photograph produced is quite small and is often difficult to read accurately. This system is still very frequently encountered in North America but is now little used in this country.

In order to produce satisfactory negatives which can be easily read and from which clear prints can be produced, the exposure (the amount of light falling on the film) must be carefully adjusted and some knowledge of photographic principles is therefore clearly desirable in any photofinish operator. This is true of all the different systems mentioned here. In the same way that a photographer using a standard camera will want to alter the length of time that a shutter remains open in order to avoid the blurring of a moving object, similar attention also needs to be given to the rate of transport of the film across the slit. There is a great difference in finishing speed between a world class sprinter and a race walker as they reach the finish and it is essential that a well-defined image is produced so that the first part of the torso may be clearly identified. The transport of the film is therefore increased to cope with the rapid movement across the slit of the sprinter whilst a very much slower speed is used for the walker's more sedate passage.

Some more sophisticated cameras using film and chemicals, (so-called "wet" cameras"), allow adjustments to be made to the temperature of both the developer and the fixer, and to the speed of extraction of the film through the chemicals in order to cope with film exposed in very poor lighting conditions. Most of the cameras have the facility to adjust the width of the slit to enhance the image when light is limited.

Film viewers, likewise, vary in complexity, some having the facility to magnify the images, valuable in the case of a very close finish, whilst many allow a print to be produced from the negative. The latter facility is particularly useful if it is felt that the Track Referee needs to be consulted before a final decision is made on the result (see below), or a record needs to be verified by a positive photograph.

The latest developments, though, have turned photofinish into a technological wonder, controlled by computers! The earlier mentioned video systems suffer from the length of time taken to scan the whole field of the screen. The lastest models utilise the slit approach long-favoured in "wet" cameras. The slit is scanned every 1/1000th of a second (or even faster) and successive scans are projected onto a high resolution monitor, producing, in effect, a continuous image of the finish line. Times are, as before, to be found along the bottom of the screen. Using this system it is possible to move the cursor

on the screen 1/1000th of a second at a time, as well as magnifying the image up to four times. The exact time of the position of the cursor line is automatically shown on the screen so that errors in reading from the time scale are eliminated. All that is required is for the operator to use the numeric key pad to type in the competitor's number and press an "Enter" key when the cursor line is on the edge of the torso and the number and time appear in a results box in the corner of the screen. To this is added the facility to produce an immediate high quality print of all or part of the finish of the race. The photograph opposite shows an example of the finished product from the 3rd IAAF World Championships in Tokyo. Rather than having a sequence number to identify the race the full title can be found at the top of the photograph. The presence of the vertical time lines should enable the reader to check the result. Using this system in Tokyo it took, on average, less than twenty seconds to produce the details of the first three in all but the very closest races. Indeed, in the case of some longer distance events, the numbers and times of the leading competitors were available for release well before the last athlete had finished the race!

Reference was made earlier to the need to position the slit in the camera exactly on the leading edge of the finish line since it is at this point that the race ends, but how is it possible to tell from the image or photograph produced from the film or monitor that the picture shows the results at the right place? In fact, this is easy to confirm. If you look carefully at the finish line on most tracks with a synthetic surface you will notice that at the intersection of the finish line and each of the individual lane lines there is a square of black paint exactly the same width as that of the lines. If you remember the principle of the slit using a "wet" camera (i.e. one using film and chemicals to develop the negative within the camera) a continuous piece of film passes in

3rd IAAF World Championships in Athletics

MEN   100m   FINAL   OFFICIAL TIMER $\mathbf{SEIKO}$

front of the minute gap. If the camera is aligned correctly the slit will be focussed on part of the black squares at the intersection of the lines. On the film these black squares will be continuously photographed and will therefore appear as a series of parallel BLACK lane lines. If the camera is not along the finish line the film will only be able to record WHITE lane lines. In the latter circumstance it is impossible to tell whether the camera is showing a position in front of or beyond the finish line and no record claim should be accepted. The fact that the IAAF

can publish a photofinish photograph of an already accepted world record in one of their publications (IAAF News Issue 4: January 1993 p. 14) which clearly shows that the camera was not aligned with the finish indicates that this fundamental aspect was not readily understood by those responsible for ratifying records!

There is an additional problem which is sometimes met when attempting to read photofinish photographs. In a very close finish where athletes are in adjacent lanes, or in a middle distance race where they are running side-by-side, it is possible for part of the body of the athlete nearest to the camera to partly obscure the body of an athlete further from the camera. It may be impossible for the exact location of the torso of the partially hidden athlete to be positively identified and the result may have to be declared as a dead-heat, in fairness to both competitors. In order to overcome this potential hazard it is usual at major Championships to place an additional camera on the inside of the track so that the finish of the race can be observed from a different angle with the likelihood that the second picture will identify the relative position of the second torso thereby enabling a correct result to be declared.

A common fallacy concerning photofinish is that its presence at a meeting makes the role of a track judge redundant. This is far from the case. In races run in lanes it should be easy enough for the photofinish operator to identify the athletes, even if it is not possible to read the numbers being worn on the hips of the runners, provided an accurate lane draw is available. In middle distance events when lanes are not operative at the finish there is both the problem of identifying athletes' leg numbers where these are obscured (or have fallen off) and of confirming that a particular athlete has completed the full distance of the race and is not going to continue for a further lap or more. In these instances it is necessary to await information on the finishing order from the Track Referee before the result can be confirmed. It is normal in a race where lapping has occurred for the camera operator to record every athlete passing the finishing post once the leader has finished, even though it may be clear that a particular athlete has been lapped. In this way if it is subsequently found that any athlete has run a lap too many it is still possible to identify the actual finishing time and position from the stored data.

A final complication should be noted. The Rules of both the IAAF and the BAF state that times obtained from photofinish pictures shall be returned to the next longer 1/100th of a second where the time recorded is not an exact 1/100th, but as has been observed, some of the latest equipment can measure to a much higher degree of accuracy. IAAF Rules recognise this situation and Rule 146.1 states that "In determining whether there has been a tie in any round for a qualifying position for the next round based on time, the Chief Photofinish Judge shall consider the actual time recorded by the competitors without regard to the Rule that the time should be read to the next longer 1/100th of a second". It is therefore permissible under IAAF Rules for an athlete to progress to the next round of a competition as a fastest loser although apparently having an identical time to another from a different heat where it is possible to identify accurately the athletes' times to a finer margin than a hundredth of a second.

One of the long-standing problems for photofinish officials has been the relationship, and relative powers, of the Chief Photofinish Judge and the Track Referee. The IAAF Rules state that the Chief Photofinish Judge "shall determine the official places of the competitors and their respective times". (IAAF Rule 121.3). Elsewhere, though, the role of the Track Referee includes the task of checking all final results and ruling on any protest or objection regarding the competition. (IAAF Rule 117.3 & 4). It appears, then, that two separate officials are given the task of confirming the result, but if there is any complaint about the result read from a photofinish picture then this has to be dealt with directly by the Track Referee and not the Chief Photofinish Judge. Remember, too, that it is only the Track Referee who can disqualify an athlete, so that the times and places read from the stored data may not be the eventual result of the race. Clearly, there needs to be close liaison between the Track Referee and the Chief Photofinish Judge.

The same problem also exists for competitions held under domestic rules, and this is why Grade 1 Track Officials are encouraged to become familiar with the operation of photofinish, ideally by working as a member of a team at a meeting since, initially, it is the Track Referee who will have to answer queries raised by protesting athletes and team managers over the result of the race. Technically, of course, the ultimate decision concerning that result remains with the Referee.

CHAPTER 6

RECORDS AND THEIR DOCUMENTATION

It is important that track officials are aware of the procedures to be adopted when a major record is established at a meeting under their control. The two main problems facing those officials would appear to be to identify which performances require a record form to be completed and which form should then be used.

The only officially recognised records are those for Seniors and for Junior Men and Women (i.e. Under 20). In the case of both Senior and Junior records the only events acceptable are those for which the IAAF recognise World Records. The current list of the events concerned is identified in the relevant domestic rule as indicated. At the time of writing these events were:-

Outdoor Records

Seniors (Rule 141.22)

Men and Women: 100m, 200m, 400m, 800m, 1000m, 1500m, 1 Mile, 2000m, 3000m, 5000m, 10000m, 20km, 1 Hour, 25km, 30km, 400m Hurdles, 4 × 100m, 4 × 200m, 4 × 400m, 4 × 800m, High Jump, Pole Vault, Long Jump, Triple Jump, Shot, Discus, Javelin, Hammer.

Men only: 110m Hurdles, 3000m Steeplechase, 4 × 1500m, 20km Walk, 2 Hours Walk, 30km Walk, 50km Walk, Decathlon.

Women only: 100m Hurdles, 5000m Walk, 10000m Walk, Heptathlon.

Juniors (i.e. Under 20) (Rule 141.23)

Men and Women: 100m, 200m, 400m, 800m, 1500m, 10000m, 400m Hurdles, 4 × 100m, 4 × 400m, High Jump, Pole Vault, Long Jump, Triple Jump, Shot, Discus, Javelin, Hammer.

Men only: 110m Hurdles, 5000m, 10000m Walk, 2000m Steeplechase, 3000m Steeplechase, Decathlon.

Women only: 100m Hurdles, 3000m, 5000m Walk, Heptathlon.

N.B. The only Junior Records officially recognised are for performances using SENIOR specifications in the throws and hurdles.

Indoor Records

Seniors only (Rule 141.24)

Men and Women: 50m, 60m, 200m, 400m, 800m, 1000m, 1500m, 1 Mile, 3000m, 5000m, 50m Hurdles, 60m Hurdles, 4 × 200m, 4 × 400m, 4 × 800m, High Jump, Pole Vault, Long Jump, Triple Jump, Shot.

Men only: 5000m Walk, Heptathlon.

Women only: 3000m Walk, Pentathlon.

Record forms need not be completed for other events or age groups.
Performances listed as "age group records" have no official standing and do not need documentation, although the National Union of Track Statisticians (NUTS) would, no doubt, welcome receipt of any information concerning the validity or otherwise of such "records".

If a National (including English, Scottish, Welsh and Northern Irish), United Kingdom All-Comers' or Commonwealth record is equalled or bettered, then the standard U.K. form should be completed. A copy of this is shown on page 46. The form requires the details of the performance of the athlete(s) and the signature, as relevant, of the Chief Timekeeper or Chief Photofinish, the Starter of the race, the Chief Walking Judge, and the Track Referee, all of whom thereby confirm the validity of the performance and their own grading within the officials' structure.

The completed form must be sent, with either a photofinish photograph or the film itself if relevant, a copy of the programme for the meeting and an official results list, to the Honorary Secretary of the BAF. In addition to these details, a record of the lap times and the leader at the commencement of each lap must also be included for events of 800m and longer. It must be appreciated that, for events up to and including 400m, only times produced from a photofinish camera are acceptable. For events longer than 400m times recorded manually by timekeepers are acceptable for records. Times recorded solely by photo-electric beams are not acceptable under any circumstances.

If a foreign athlete establishes a National Record and requires documentation to support this, a standard UK form could be used, but the form shown on page 47 has been specially designed for this purpose and requires only two signatures, that of the Referee and a representative of the National Association, to verify the qualifications of the officials concerned and the status of the track.

For European and World Records, the appropriate IAAF World Record form must be completed. (Note that there are different forms for records set by Seniors and Juniors, and for those set indoors and outdoors).

British Athletic Federation

U.K. All-Comers   U.K. National   U.K. Junior   Other record (please specify)..
(Reference should be made to B.A.F. Rule 141 : I.A.A.F. Rule 148)

1.   Event...Indoors/Outdoor   2.   Date.......................................
3.   Performance...   4.   Meeting...............................
5.   Venue...   6.   Wind Reading.....................
7.   Name of competitor...
                                 First Name   Surname
8.   Date of Birth..   9.   Place of Birth.....................
10.   Club/Country..

For Relay Events details are required of the team in running order:-
1...   2..
3...   4..

TIMEKEEPERS' CERTIFICATE
Complete section 1 <u>or</u> 2 as appropriate:

1.   A fully automatic, correctly aligned, electrical timing device, was used. I confirm the time above.

Name of Photo-finish Chief...Signature...........................
or
2.   We certify that we were official timekeepers of the above event and that the exact time recorded on our watches for the competitor concerned was:

Time	Signature	Name	Grade

I confirm that the official time for the competitor named was..

Name of Chief Timekeeper...Signature...................................Grade....................

STARTER'S CERTIFICATE
I certify that the start of the race was in accordance with the relevant Rules.

Name of Starter...Signature...................................Grade....................

WALKING JUDGE'S CERTIFICATE
I certify that I was Chief Judge of Walking for the above event and that the competitor concerned complied with the definition of walking under B.A.F./I.A.A.F. Rules and that this was confirmed by three suitably qualified Judges of Walking.

Name of Chief Judge...Signature...................................Grade....................

DOPING CONTROL CERTIFICATE
(Not necessary for U.K. All-Comers Records unless performance is also U.K. National, European or World Record)
I certify that the above mentioned competitor(s) provided a sample for drug testing in accordance with Rule 24 and Appendix B of the B.A.F. Rules for Competition.

Name of Official...Signature...
Status...

REFEREE'S CERTIFICATE
I certify that all the conditions as laid down by B.A.F./I.A.A.F. Rules for Competition were complied with and that the performance was made in bona fide competition in accordance with these Rules. The following information is attached:-
1.   A schedule giving lap times and the name of the leader for each lap.
2.   A copy of the photo-finish picture.
3.   A copy of the Field Event scorecard which shows the grade of the officials for the event.
4.   A copy of the programme of the meeting.

Name of Referee..Signature...................................Grade....................

British Athletic Federation

RECORD OF PERFORMANCE

Event .... Meeting ....

Performance ....

Venue .... Date ....

Wind-speed and direction ....

Competitor's name (BLOCK CAPITALS) ....
(First Names)   (Surname)

For relay events, please enter the name of the team above and the names of the athletes below, **in the order of running:**

(1) ....

(2) ....

(3) ....

(4) ....

PHOTO/SCORE CARD ENCLOSED

Referee's Certificate

I certify that the performance claimed was achieved in bona-fide competition held in accordance with I.A.A.F. Rules. The Judges and Officials controlling the event were properly qualified and approved by my National Association. The equipment used was verified and conforms with I.A.A.F. Specifications.

Signature of Referee ....

Certificate of National Association

As the authorised representative of the ....
I certify that the statements recorded above are fully authentic.

The stadium facilities (track, runways, throwing-circles and landing areas) have been properly surveyed, and conform with I.A.A.F. specifications in all respects.

Signed .... Date ....

47

CHAPTER 7

BRITISH ATHLETIC FEDERATION OFFICIALS' GRADING SCHEME

The BAF operates the scheme for the testing and grading of officials within the United Kingdom through its Officials' Committee which has the direct responsibility for maintaining the high standards and reputation of British officiating both domestically and internationally.

Officials may become qualified in track and field in one or more of four categories:–

(a) Track   (c) Timekeeping
(b) Field   (d) Starting/Marking

Track Judges

Grade 4

This is the initial grade which is attained by passing the Preliminary Written Test. (Pass mark 65%)

These tests are arranged by County/District/Services Associations, often after a series of talks by prominent officials, but it should be noted that these simple written tests require some elementary practical knowledge of judging as well as a sound grasp of the main rules.

Lists of officials who have qualified within the Grade are maintained by the appropriate County/District/Services Association.

Grade 3 (County Level)

For promotion to Grade 3 status an official must have had at least one year's experience as a Grade 4 judge, and have been given **at least one satisfactory written report by an experienced, higher graded official**. A list of the meetings at which the candidate has officiated during the year must be received by

the County/District/Services Association in order for upgrading to be approved. Again, the list of officials in this grade is maintained by the appropriate County/District/Services Association.

Grade 2 (Regional Level)

To progress to this grade an official must have had considerable experience as a Grade 3 judge for a **minimum of two years**, and have been given **at least** two good written reports from different experienced, higher graded officials. A record of the meetings attended over the previous two years must be supplied to the relevant Officials' Secretary. Upgrading in the minimum time shown will only be accorded to an outstanding candidate, as evidenced both by the content of the reports and by the scope of the list of meetings attended. The Regional and National Associations (i.e. Midland Counties, North of England, South of England, Northern Ireland, Scotland and Wales) maintain the list of their officials at this grade. These lists are used to select officials for Regional and National Association Championships and representative matches.

Grade 1 (International Level)

For promotion to Grade 1 an official must have had **at least three years'** experience as a Grade 2 Judge. This experience would need to include a large number of meetings attended over the previous three years, and an indication that several of these were of an appropriately high standard. In addition, the Advanced Written Test must be successfully completed. The invitation to sit the Advanced Test is made by the appropriate Regional or National Association Committee. When a pass mark is achieved in that Test upgrading may then be considered, provided the candidate receives **at least three**

good reports from **experienced and active higher graded officials (ideally Referees)**. At least **two of these reports must relate to the previous season.** The successful candidate is also expected to have had experience operating as Track Clerk of the Course. Upgrading in the minimum time indicated will only be accorded to an outstanding candidate as evidenced by the reports and the list of duties undertaken.

The Grade 1 list of officials is maintained by the Federation's Officials' Committee and forms the basis for selection for the staffing of international meetings held in the United Kingdom.

Grade 1 (Referee) (International Referee Level)

Officials from within Grade 1 may be invited to become Grade 1 (Referees) provided they have:–

(i) **At least three years' varied and extensive experience within Grade 1** to include:–
    (a) National and International meetings as a judge, and
    (b) a considerable amount of experience as Referee at Regional Championships or meetings of a similar standard.

(ii) Excellent written reports on the candidate **operating as a Referee** from **at least three active officials of Referee grade.**

(iii) The ability to produce a correct result from a photofinish image.

Officials appointed to this Grade are immediately considered capable of acting as Track Referee at an International meeting.

The list of Grade 1 (Referees) is maintained by the Federation's Officials' Committee.

As will have been noticed, at each stage in the progression through the grading system accurate lists of the meetings attended must be maintained by the official concerned. These lists will be reviewed when the requirement of suitable experience is being considered, and **no upgrading will be achieved without this information.** Standard forms for recording such experience are available and need to be submitted annually to the Officials' Committee relevant to the Grade (i.e. County or Region).

Full details of the syllabus content for both the Preliminary and Advanced Written Tests can be found in Appendix E of the current edition of the British Athletic Federation's Rules for Competition. This Appendix also provides additional information on the Grading Scheme for officials.

NOTES

Database typeset by BPC Whitefriars Ltd.
Printed and bound by BPC Blackpool Ltd., both members of The British Printing Company Ltd.